Islam For Teenagers

By
Abu Zayd Kamran Ali

ISBN: 9798849546971

First printing edition 2022.

INTRODUCTION

All praise is due to Allah, and Allah's Peace and Blessings be upon His Final Messenger, his family, his noble Companions, and all those who follow them with righteousness until the Day of Judgment.

I have decided on 'Islam For Teenagers' as a title for the present book. I felt a need to present this small but informative book to our young readers for the purpose of providing knowledge & rulings on several topics.

- Problems faced by teenagers in their daily lives.
- Questions asked by a lot of Muslim teenagers.
- Issues parents are hesitant or negligent to address.

My advice to every Muslim teenager is to make your intention sincere, practice what you learn, do not kill (waste) hours viewing corrupt media, listening to music, gossiping and being lazy. Rather you should occupy your time with the Kitaab of Allah, memorizing and reciting it. Busy your life with beneficial knowledge, educational family sittings and fruitful discussions.

I hope you will find value in reading this book. I've tried to cover the important topics a Muslim teenager can easily understand.

Author:
Abu Zayd Kamran Ali
Date: September 2, 2022

Table of Contents

ARROGANCE

Definition: **rejecting the truth and looking down on people.**

Arrogance: A belief in one's own greatness above the people, and possession of virtue over them.

Self-conceit: Looking at one's own actions and becoming amazed by them; regarding them as great and lofty.

So, self-conceit describes one's actions while arrogance describes one's soul. Both traits are dispraised.

Arrogance is of two types: Arrogance toward the truth and arrogance toward people.

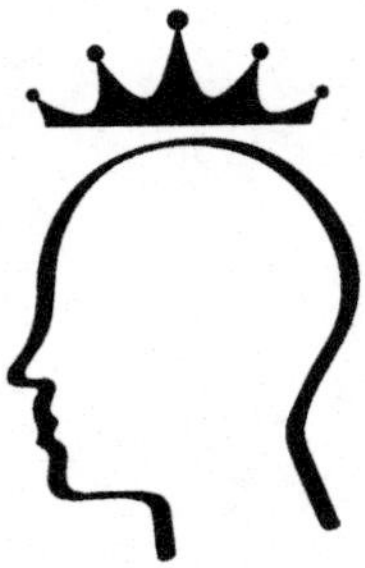

The Prophet ﷺ clarified both in his statement,

"Arrogance is to reject the truth and to belittle the people"

Muslim collected it in Kitaabul Emaan under the chapter "The prohibition of arrogance and its clarification".

The meaning behind the statement, **"reject the truth"** is to discard it, be averse to it, and to deny it; and the meaning behind the statement, **"belittle the people"** is to disparage and disdain them, and deem people to be of no worth, seeing oneself above them.

The Prophet's ﷺ statement, **"reject the truth"** means discarding the truth and not accepting it; because of thinking highly of oneself and one's opinion. He views himself greater than the truth, Allah forbid. The sign of such is that evidences from the Book and Sunnah are brought before him yet he will not accept them; instead persisting in his stubbornness. This is the exact description of rejecting the truth, Allah forbid.

Taken from the book:
The Prohibition of Arrogance & Self-Conceit
Shaykh Muhammad Ibn Saleh Al-Uthaymeen

Imaam ash-Shaafi'i said:
The person with the highest status (amongst the people) is the one who does not see his status, and the person with the most virtue is the one who does not see his virtue.

Siyar 'Alaam an-Nubalaa 10/99

Yusuf bin Isbaat was asked: What is the height of humility? He said: ”You do not meet anyone except that you consider him more virtuous than yourself.”

Siyar 'Alaam an-Nubalaa 9/170

Ibn al-Qayyim said:
And from the signs of wellbeing and success is that whenever the slave is increased in his knowledge, he increases in humility and mercy; and whenever he is increased in action, he increases in his fear and caution; and whenever his age is increased, he decreases in eagerness; and whenever he is increased in wealth, he increases in his generosity and spending; and whenever his status and honor is increased, he increases in coming close to the people, in fulfilling their needs and being humble in (their presence).

And the signs of wretchedness are: Whenever he is increased in knowledge, he increases in pride and haughtiness; and whenever he is increased in actions, he increases in his boasting, mockery of the people and having a good opinion of himself; and whenever he is increased in his status and honor, he increases in pride and haughtiness. These affairs of (wellbeing and wretchedness) are a trial and a test from Allah, by which He puts His slaves to trial. He brings about wellbeing and wretchedness to a people by way of these affairs.

[Al-Fawaa-id. Page:228]

BACKBITING & SLANDERING

Definition: **to mention your brother (in his absence) in a way he dislikes.**

Abu Huraira reported: The Messenger of Allah ﷺ said, "Do you know what backbiting is?" They said, "Allah and his messenger know best." The Prophet ﷺ said, **"To mention your brother in a way he dislikes."** It was said, "What do you think if what I said about him is true?" The Prophet ﷺ said, **"If what you say about him is true, it is backbiting. If it is not true, it is slander."**

Source: Saheeh Muslim, 2589.

Explanation:
As for Backbiting (Gheebah), then it is when you mention something about a person (in his absence), that he hates (to have mentioned), whether it is about: His body, his religious characteristics, his worldly affairs, his self, his physical appearance, his character, his wealth, his child, his father, his wife, his servant, his slave, his turban, his attire, his manner of walking, his smile, his dissoluteness, his frowning, his cheerfulness or anything else related to the above. Likewise, it is the same whether you mention that about him with words, through writings, or whether you point or indicate him by gesturing with your eyes, hand or head.

As for the body, then it is when you say: "he is blind", "he limps", "he is bleary-eyed", "he is bald", "he is short", "he is tall", "he is black", "he is yellow". As for his religious qualities, then it is when you say: "he is a sinner", "he is a thief", "he is a betrayer", "he is an oppressor", "he takes the prayer lightly", "he is lenient with impurities", "he does not behave well towards his parents", "he does not pay the Zakaah duly", and "he does not avoid backbiting." As for the worldly matters, then it is when you say: "he has poor manners", "he's unmindful of people", "he does not think that anyone has a right over him", "he talks too much", "he eats and sleeps too much", "he sleeps at the wrong times", "he sits in places he does not belong in."

As for those matters connected with one's parents, then it is when you say: "his father is a sinner", "a Nabatean", "a Negro", "a loafer", "a seedsman", "a cattle dealer", "a carpenter", "a blacksmith", "a weaver." As for his character, then it is when you say: "he has bad manners", "he is arrogant", "he is quarrelsome", "he is rash and hasty", "he is tyrannical", "he is feeble", "he has a weak heart", "he is irresponsible", "he is dismal", "he is dissolute", etc. As for the garment: "it has wide sleeves", "it has short hems", "what a filthy garment", and so on.

Book Source: Guarding the Tongue
By Imaam Al-Nawawi

Some of the most common remarks we hear around us:

Allah, the Exalted, says: "Not a word does he (or she) utter but there is a watcher by him ready (to record it)."

[Surah Qaaf, verse 18]

BEARD & HAIRCUTS

BEARD

Growing the beard is Waajib (mandatory) for all males who are capable of doing so. As will be presented below, there is ample evidence for this in the Ahadeeth (narrations), and it is the unanimous opinion of the scholars of Islam.

The Muslims have been commanded to be different and distinct from the disbelievers. In Surat ul-Faatihah, we are commanded to ask Allah to guide us away from the ways of the disbelievers:

"Guide us to the Straight Path - The path of those upon whom You have bestowed Your favor, not of those who have earned Your anger, nor of those who are astray." *[Al-Faatihah 1:6~7]*

Narrated Ibn `Umar:

Allah's Messenger ﷺ said, "Cut the mustaches short and leave the beard.

Saheeh Al-Bukhaari 5893.

LENGTH OF THE BEARD

Ibn Umar reported: The Prophet ﷺ said, "Be different from the idolaters. Let the beard grow and trim the mustache." Whenever Ibn Umar, performed the Hajj or Umrah pilgrimage, he would grab hold of his beard and cut what was beyond his grasp.

Source: Saheeh Al-Bukhaari 5553, Sahih Muslim 259.

Non-Islamic Beard Styles

Islamic beards should not be confused with some beard styles. The examples below are designed and trimmed to look like the latest **fashion** and **trend**.

Examples of some Non-Islamic Mustache Styles which are in direct contradiction to the Sunnah

The best is to trim the mustache as is the Sunnah. As for shaving it, that is not Sunnah. The analogy drawn by some of them, that it is prescribed to shave it as the head is shaved in Hajj is an analogy when a clear text states something else, so this analogy does not carry any weight. Hence Maalik said concerning shaving the mustache: It is an innovation that has appeared among the people, but we should not turn away from what is mentioned in the Sunnah, because following it is guidance, righteousness, happiness and success. End quote.

Shaykh Ibn 'Uthaymeen said in Majmoo' al-Fataawa (11/Baab al-Siwaak wa Sunan al-Fitrah/question no. 54)

The Saheeh ahaadeeth from the Messenger of Allah ﷺ indicate that it is prescribed to trim the mustache. For example, the Prophet ﷺ said: "Trim the mustache and let the beard grow; be different from the mushrikeen." (Bukhaari & Muslim).

And he ﷺ said: "Trim the mustache and let the beard grow; be different from the Magians," and in some versions it says: "Trim the mustache." Trimming means cutting it very short. The one who cuts his mustache very short so that the upper lip is visible or trims it is not to blame, because the Ahaadeeth mention two things, but it is not permissible to leave the edges of the mustache, rather the whole mustache should be trimmed or cut, in accordance with the Sunnah. End quote.

Shaykh 'Abd al-'Azeez ibn Baaz, Shaykh 'Abd al-Razzaaq 'Afeefi, Shaykh 'Abd-Allah ibn Qa'ood.

Fataawa al-Lajnah al-Daa'imah (5/149).

Examples of some Haraam Haircuts

One of the issues that many people, particularly the youth, have been confronted with in recent years is their insatiable desire to follow **Western fashion** and compete to be up-to-date with society's latest trends. They want people to notice that they are dressed in the most up-to-date fashions and have the most fashionable haircuts. They imitate well-known sinners and disbelievers in society, such as singers, musicians, actors, sports personalities, fashion models, and celebrities in order to be fashionable. Some of our Muslim brothers and sisters may be unaware of the Sharee'ah rulings on clothing, hairstyles, and resembling the Kuffaar, while others may be aware but overwhelmed by the desire to fit in or keep up.

Qaza' means shaving part of the head and leaving part of it. It is of different types:

1- Where the shaving is not done properly, so some hair is shaved on the right side and on the left, and on the front, and on the back [i.e., separate parts of the head are shaved and the rest is left].

2- Where the middle is shaved and the sides are left.

3- Where the sides are shaved and the middle is left.

4- Where the front part only is shaved and the rest is left.

By Shaykh Ibn 'Uthaymeen in al-Sharh al-Mumti' (1/167).

Shaykh Ibn 'Uthaymeen said:
Qaza' is Makrooh, because the Prophet ﷺ saw a boy, part of whose hair had been shaved and part had been left. He told them not to do that and said: "Shave it all or leave it all." But if it is done in imitation of the Kuffaar it is Haraam, because imitating the Kuffaar is Haraam. The Prophet ﷺ said: "Whoever imitates a people is one of them." end quote.

Al-Sharh al-Mumti' (1/167).

FOR MEN — KEEPING ONE'S HAIR AND LEAVING IT TO GROW

Indeed, keeping one's hair and leaving it to grow must meet certain requirements, among which are:
There must be sincerity to Allah, the Most High and following of the guidance of the Prophet ﷺ in order to attain reward and merit.

There should be no imitation of women in his leaving of the hair to grow, such that he does with his hair what the women do with their hair, from the aspects of beautification that is specific to them.

He should not desire by it to imitate the People of the Book or anyone else among the idol worshippers. Or in imitation of the haircuts and hairstyles of sinful Muslims, such as music and film artists or whoever treads their way, such as the shameless ones among the sports figures.

One should clean it and groom it every other day. And it is recommended to oil it, perfume it and split it down the middle of the head. And if it grows long, then one can put it in locks. *Fataawa of Shaykh Al-Albaani*

From Al-Asaalah Magazine Issues 1-21, Translated and Arranged by: Isma'eel Alarcon

CAN WOMEN CUT THEIR HAIR SHORT?

Imaam Muslim narrated in his Saheeh that the wives of the Prophet ﷺ used to cut their hair so that it came down no lower than their earlobes.

But if a woman cuts her hair too short, so that it looks like a man's hair, then this is undoubtedly Haraam, because the Prophet ﷺ cursed women who resemble men.

Similarly, if she cuts it in a style that resembles the hairstyles of disbelieving women and immoral women, then whoever imitates a people is one of them.

But if she only cuts it a little, so that it does not go to the extent of resembling men's hairstyles, and does not resemble the hairstyles of immoral women and disbelieving women, then there is nothing wrong with that." End quote.

(Fataawa Noor 'ala ad-Darb (Fataawa az-Zeenah wa'l-Marah/Qass ash-Sha'r)

BULLYING

Definition: **bullying is the use of force, hurtful teasing or threat, to abuse, aggressively dominate or intimidate.**

The bully relies on his physical might, as well as his "gang" of friends. He also takes advantage of his victim's weakness or being on his own.

This problem is common in schools, neighborhoods, among siblings, family members and so on. It frequently results in the victim suffering serious physical and psychological trauma. If no one is informed of the victim's everyday suffering, it may drive him to commit suicide.

What all parents must do is strengthen their children's religious commitment and raise them with sound creed and positive characteristics such as tolerance, respect, good manners, love of others, and a desire to help and cooperate, among others.

WHAT IS FAMILY BULLYING?

Bullying, contrary to popular belief, does not always fade away with the acne, driving lessons, and standardized tests of adolescence. In fact, it can be found in almost any setting and can last into adulthood.

Adults can be bullied in their families, in addition to online bullying, workplace bullying, and even sibling bullying. Any family member can be a bully, and any family member can be a target.

A sibling, a parent, an aunt, an uncle, a grandparent, an adult child, or even one of your in-laws could be the bully in your family. If you have a family member who is a bully, here's what you need to know to deal with the situation.

Family bullying usually takes the form of relational aggression, but it can also escalate into physical bullying in extreme cases. Family bullies, on the other hand, frequently use manipulation, humiliation, and intimidation.

They may also be relentless in their criticism, frequently blaming the target, calling them names, and refusing to value or appreciate them. A family bully may even use gaslighting or the silent treatment to isolate the target by turning other family members against them or isolating them.

Bullying in the family occurs because the adult who bullies has never learned how to interact with others in a healthy manner. Sometimes it happens because the bully is attempting to manipulate and control the situation.

It was narrated that Anas said: The Messenger of Allah ﷺ said: "Help your brother whether he is a wrongdoer or is wronged." A man said: "O Messenger of Allah, I can help him if he is wronged but what if he is the wrongdoer, how can I help him?" He said: "Stop him or prevent him from doing wrong. That is how you help him."

Narrated by al-Bukhaari (6952).

BULLYING IS AN ACT OF OPPRESSION

Bullying is "**repeated oppression**, psychological or physical, of a less powerful person by a more powerful person".

"Indeed, Allah orders justice and good conduct and giving to relatives and forbids immorality and bad conduct and **oppression**. He admonishes you that perhaps you will be reminded."

(Surah An-Nahl, 16:90).

Prophet ﷺ said, "Beware of the supplication of the **oppressed**, for there is no barrier between it and Allah."

Al-Bukhaari, 4090.

TYPES OF BULLYING

Researchers have discovered that there is a lot more to it than meets the eye. Many people used to believe that bullying was limited to physical abuse and name-calling. Bullying can take many forms, from excluding and gossiping about people to making fun of their race or religion.

➊PHYSICAL, Hitting, Pinching, Hair Pulling, Kicking, Tripping, Pushing, Blocking.

➋VERBAL, Name-Calling, Insults, Teasing, Intimidation, Racist Remarks or Verbal Abuse.

➌SOCIAL, designed to embarrass or humiliate someone, it can include lying and spreading rumors, encouraging others to socially exclude someone, mimicking unkindly, or acting nasty to embarrass or humiliate them.

➍CYBER, it occurs through the use of digital technology, such as computers and smartphones, as well as software such as social media, instant messaging, texts, websites, and other platforms, and can include abusive or hurtful texts, emails, posts, images or video, gossip, and rumors.

CLOTHING & ACCESSORIES

Forbidden Types of Clothing:

❶ Clothing that reveals the private parts:
Muslims are required to cover their intimate parts with appropriate clothing. The Qur'aan says, "Children of Adam! We have sent down clothing to you to conceal your private parts ..." (Soorat Al-Aʿraaf, 7:26).

For both men and women, Islam has established modesty standards. The minimum amount of skin to be covered for men is between the navel and the knee. Women must cover their bodies except for their faces and hands when they are in the company of men who are not related to them.

Clothing must also be loose enough to cover the body properly, according to Islam. As a result, skintight and see-through clothing are prohibited in Islam. In fact, the Prophet ﷺ issued a warning to those who do not dress modestly, stating that there are "two types of people who will be punished in Hellfire," one of whom is "women who appear to be naked despite being dressed."

❷ Clothing that involves dressing like or imitating the opposite gender:

This type of clothing is strictly forbidden in Islam, and wearing it is considered one of the major sins. It was narrated that Abu Hurayrah said: The Messenger of

Allah ﷺ cursed the man who wears women's clothing and the woman who wears men's clothing.

Narrated by Abu Dawood (4098) and classed as saheeh by al-Nawawi in al-Majmoo' (4/469) and by al-Albaani in Saheeh Abi Dawood.

It was narrated from Ibn 'Abbaas that the Prophet ﷺ cursed men who imitate women and women who imitate men, and he said: "Throw them out of your houses."

Al-Bukhaari, 5885.

❸ Silk clothing or clothing adorned with gold silk for men: Referring to gold and silk once, the Prophet ﷺ said, "These are forbidden for men among my followers but permissible for women."

(Sunan Ibn Maajah: 3595; Sunan Abu Dawood: 4057).

BRACELETS FOR MEN

Men who wear bracelets & strings around their wrists?

Answer: This is Haraam for males, it is imitation of women. The wearing of bracelets is something specific for women – males are not to wear them. The Messenger invoked the curse upon the men who resemble and imitate women, and likewise the women who resemble and imitate men.

(Answered by: Shaykh Saaleh Al-Fawzaan)

RED COLOR FOR MEN

It is permissible to wear red clothes if the red is combined with another color; it is not permissible to wear plain red, because the Prophet ﷺ forbade doing so.

From al-Baraa' who said: "The Messenger of Allah ﷺ had hair down to his earlobes. I saw him wearing a red Hullah, and I have never seen anyone more handsome than him."

(Abu Dawood, no. 4072; Ibn Maajah, no. 3599. Classed as Saheeh by al-Albaani – Saheeh Sunan Abi dawood, 768).

What is meant by a red Hullah is a suit of two Yemeni garments which are woven with red and black stripes, or red and green stripes. It is described as red because of the red stripes in it.

This is the view of a number of scholars, such as al-Haafiz Ibn Hajar (Fath al-Baari Sharh 'ala Saheeh al-Bukhaari, no. 5400) and Ibn al-Qayyim (Zaad al-Ma'aad, 1-137).

SUMMARY

For women when in public among unrelated (non-mahram) men:

- Clothing must cover the entire body except for the face and hands when in the company of non-related males.
- Clothing must be loose, so the shape of the body is not seen.
- Thick enough so that it is not see-through.
- Should not resemble the clothing of men.
- Should not be showy or gaudy.

For men:

- Clothing must conceal whatever is between the naval and knee.
- Must be loose, and not see-through, so that the private areas remain concealed (by loose, not tight garments).
- All garments must be above the ankle bone.
- Should not resemble the clothing of women.
- They should not resemble something that merely seeks to imitate un-Islamic practices/fashions (e.g. clothing of Buddhists, priests, rabbis, hip-hop artists, movie stars, etc.)
- It cannot be made of silk, plain red colored or dyed with saffron.

WIGS & EXTENSIONS

Narrated Abu Huraira:
The Prophet ﷺ said, "Allah has cursed the lady who artificially lengthens (her or someone else's) hair and the one who gets her hair lengthened and the one who tattoos (herself or someone else) and the one who gets herself tattooed"

Al-Bukhaari, 5933.
Book 77, Hadith 14

Question: What is the ruling regarding a woman having hair extensions?

Response: It is Haraam for a woman to have hair extensions using (real) hair or that which resembles (real) hair for the authentic evidences which mention this (prohibition).

And with Allah lies all success and may Allah send prayers and salutations upon our Prophet ﷺ and his family and his companions.

The Permanent Committee for Islamic Research and Fataawa
Fataawa al-Lajnah ad-Daa.imah lil-Buhooth al-'Ilmiyyah wal-Iftaa., – Volume 5, Page 193, Question 10 of Fatwa No.9850;
Fataawa wa Ahkaam fee Sha'r an-Nisaa – Question 5, Page 8

COMPANIONS & FRIENDS

Definition: **a companion is a person who frequently spends time with you, associates with you, or accompanies you when you go places.**

One of the greatest things that help Muslims to have piety and uprightness on the path of truth and guidance is keeping the company of good people and avoiding evil company, for man, by his nature, gets influenced by his friends and companions and adopts their characters and manners.

Narrated Abu Hurayrah:
The Prophet ﷺ said: A man follows the religion of his friend; so, each one should consider whom he makes his friend.

Sunan Abi Dawud 4833, Graded Hasan by Al-Albaani

This means that he takes on the habits of his friend, and his path and his lifestyle, "so pay attention..." meaning, reflect and ponder over who you're taking as your friend. So, if you are pleased with his Religion and character, befriend him and if not, keep away from him.

The best companion is the one who is pious, righteous, possesses noble conduct and manners.

Whoever is fortunate enough to have a companion with these attributes, he must therefore hold fast to him, fulfill his right of companionship and be truthful with him. He should also respect him, share with him his happy and sad moments, assist him in hardship and overlook his mistakes, because no man is free of errors and mistakes and it is enough an honor for a man that his faults are at least countable.

The worst of all companions is the one who is weak and corrupt religiously, evil in conduct, nothing good is said of his behavior. He is concerned only with achieving his desires.

The teenage brain has lots of plasticity, which means it can change, adapt and respond to its environment. So, keep away from friends who accustom you to obscene talk, instigate you to commit immoral acts, waste your time in useless amusements, wasteful spending and other forbidden things.

In the teenage years, young people often spend much more time with friends and less time with parents. Not all friendships are positive or good for children. Among teenagers, negative relationships are sometimes called 'toxic friendships'. Muslim parents are therefore obliged before anybody else to take good care of their children, nurture them on Islamic teachings and manners and protect them from bad company and means that lead to evil in order that they may be good children and prosper in this world and the next. Parents, by doing so, will be doing what Allah has made obligatory on them.

CURSING & SWEARING

The Prophet ﷺ did not swear, curse (cuss), use profane language, or spread obscenity. Rather, he warned us about such language and he counseled us to uphold the integrity and dignity of the believer by avoiding such behavior.

Abdullah ibn Mas'ood reported: The Messenger of Allah ﷺ said: None has more self-respect than Allah, so He has made **obscenities unlawful.**

Al-Bukhaari, 4847.

Abu Huraira reported: The Messenger of Allah ﷺ said: It is not befitting the truthful that they **curse** others.

Saheeh Muslim, 2597.

Aisha reported: The Messenger of Allah ﷺ said: Your duty is to be gentle and **beware of harshness & indecency.**

Al-Bukhaari, 5683.

Anas ibn Malik reported:
The Prophet ﷺ would not abuse others, he would not use obscene words, and he would not curse others. If he wanted to admonish anyone of us, he used to say: *What is wrong with him? His forehead be dusted!*

Al-Bukhaari, 5684.

Abdullah ibn Mas'ood reported: The Messenger of Allah ﷺ said: The believer does not taunt others, he does not curse others, he does not use profanity, and he does not abuse others.

Sunan At-Tirmidhi 1977, Grade: Hasan.

Abdullah ibn Amr reported: The Messenger of Allah ﷺ said: Verily, one of the worst sins is that a man curses his own parents.

It was said, "O Messenger of Allah, how can a man curse his own parents?" The Prophet said: He abuses the father of another man and then that man abuses his father and mother.

Al-Bukhaari, 5628.

DRAWING & PHOTOGRAPHY

Question: What type of pictures are permitted to draw?

Narrated by Saeed bin Abu Al Hasan:
While I was with Ibn 'Abbas a man came and said, "O father of 'Abbas! My sustenance is from my manual profession and I make these pictures." Ibn 'Abbas said, "I will tell you only what I heard from Allah's Apostle. I heard him saying, 'Whoever makes a picture will be punished by Allah till he puts life in it, and he will never be able to put life in it.' " Hearing this, that man heaved a sigh and his face turned pale. Ibn 'Abbas said to him, "What a pity! If you insist on making pictures, I advise you to make pictures of trees and any other inanimate objects."

Al-Bukhaari, 3428.

Inanimate objects are **items that are not alive**. They can be anything from a rock to a book, and do not have any life in them.

The Prophet ﷺ said, "The Angels (of Mercy) do not enter a house wherein there is a picture."

Al-Bukhaari 3226, Book 59, Hadeeth 37.

Praying in places where these images are is not permissible except in cases of necessity. The same applies to praying in clothes on which there are images of animals; it is not permissible, but if he does it, his prayer is sound but he is committing a Haraam action.

Fataawa al-Lajnah al-Daa'imah, 1/705.

PHOTOGRAPHY

The Prophet ﷺ said:
"Those who make these pictures [of living things] will be punished on the Day of Resurrection, and it will be said to them. 'Bring to life what you have made.'"

(Al-Bukhaari, 5951, Muslim, 2108).

Shaykh Ibn 'Uthaymeen said:
"It may be obligatory to make images sometimes, especially moving images. For example, if we see someone committing a crime that is a crime against a person's rights, such as a murder attempt and the like, and it cannot be proven except by means of a picture, then in that case taking a picture is obligatory, especially in cases where pictures could tell the full story, because the means are subject to the same rulings as the ends. If we use this image-making to prove the identity of a person lest he is accused of a crime committed by someone else, there is nothing wrong with this either, rather it is essential. But if we take a picture in order to enjoy looking at it, this is undoubtedly Haraam."

Ash-Sharh al-Mumti' (2/197-199).

DRUG & ALCOHOL

There is no doubt that taking drugs is Haraam, including hashish, opium, cocaine, morphine, and so on.

The Prophet ﷺ said: "Every intoxicant is Khamr, and every intoxicant is Haraam. Whoever drinks Khamr in this world and dies persisting in that and without having repented, will not drink it in the Hereafter."

Saheeh Muslim, 2003.

Al-Haafiz ibn Hajar said: The general meaning of the words, "Every intoxicant is Haraam," is taken as evidence that whatever causes intoxication is Haraam, even if it is not a drink. So that includes hashish and other things. Al-Nawawi and others were certain that it is an intoxicant, and others were certain that dulls the senses, and it is arrogant to say otherwise, because its visible effects are the same as those of Khamr, such as euphoria and addiction.

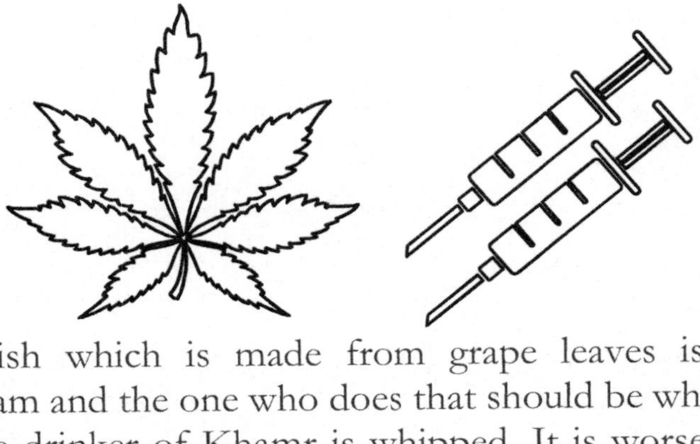

Hashish which is made from grape leaves is also Haraam and the one who does that should be whipped as the drinker of Khamr is whipped. It is worse than

Khamr in a way, because it corrupts the mind and mood, robs a man of his masculinity, and makes him heedless about his honor, and other evil consequences. End quote.

Ibn Taymiyyah, al-Siyaasah al-Shar'iyyah (p. 92).

Shaykh al-Islam Ibn Taymiyah said:
Everything that takes away one's senses is Haraam, even if it does not result in drunkenness or intoxication. If it takes away the senses it is Haraam according to the consensus of the Muslims.

The scholars who studied the issue realized that hashish is an intoxicant, and that it is only consumed by evildoers, because of the pleasure and euphoria it brings. So, it is like intoxicating drinks. Khamr makes a person lively and argumentative, whereas hashish makes him relaxed and lethargic, but it still befogs the mind and opens the door to physical desires and heedlessness with regard to one's honor, which makes it worse than intoxicating drinks. This is something that was introduced by the Tatars.

The one who consumes a little or a lot of it is to be subjected to the punishment for drinking: eighty or forty lashes, if he is a Muslim who believes that intoxicants are Haraam. End quote.

al-Fataawa al-Kubra, 3/423.

ALCOHOL

Al-Haarith reported: Uthmaan ﷺ said, "Stay away from alcohol, for it is the mother of all evil. By Allah, faith and addiction to wine cannot be combined but that one of them will eventually expel the other."

Sunan al-Nasa'i, 5666.
Grade: Saheeh (authentic) according to Al-Albaani

Narrated by Ibn 'Umar: The Messenger of Allah ﷺ said: "Allah has cursed alcohol, the one who drinks it, the one who pours it, the one who sells it, the one who buys it, the one who squeezes (the grapes, etc.), the one for whom it is squeezed, the one who carries it and the one to whom it is carried."

Abu Dawood (3674) and Ibn Maajah (3380).
Classed as Saheeh by al-Albaani.

FREE MIXING

The Law of Islam (Sharee'ah) prohibits men and women from meeting, mixing, and intermingling in one place, from crowding them together, and from revealing and exposing women to men. These actions are forbidden because they are among the causes of fitnah (temptation or trial with negative consequences), arousing desires, and committing indecency and wrongdoing.

Shaykh 'Abul Aziz ibn Baaz mentioned: That the women in the time of the Prophet ﷺ did not intermingle with the men, not in the Masaajid or in the market places. This is from the types of intermingling that people who desire rectification have forbidden even in these times. The Qur'aan and the Sunnah and scholars of the Ummah warn against this as a caution from falling into fitnah, tribulation, and corruption in society.

Imaam ibn Qayyim continues: That there is no doubt that allowing the intermingling of women with men is the root of tribulation and evil in societies. It is from the foremost reasons for the descent of the punishment of Allah upon the people, and it is a cause for the general corruption in society.

The Prophet ﷺ enforced separation of men and women even at Allah's most revered and preferred place, the mosque. This was accomplished via the separation of the women's rows from the men's; men were asked to stay in the mosque after completion of the obligatory prayer so that women will have enough time to leave the mosque; and, a special door was assigned to women. Evidence of the foregoing are:

Umm Salamah said that after Allah's Messenger ﷺ said "as-Salamu 'Alaykum wa Rahmatullah' twice announcing the end of the prayer, women would stand up and leave. He would stay for a while before leaving. Ibn Shihab said that he thought that the staying of the Prophet ﷺ was in order for the women to be able to leave before the men who wanted to depart."

Al-Bukhaari, 793.

GAMES & SPORTS

Abu Hurayrah reported: The Messenger of Allah ﷺ said: "**The strong believer is better and more beloved to Allah than the weak believer, although both are good.**"

Saheeh Muslim, 2664.

SWIMMING

It is narrated from the Prophet ﷺ that he said: "Everything in which there is no remembrance of Allah is idle play, except four things: a man playing with his wife; a man training his horse; a man running between two lines (as in a race); and a man learning how to swim."

Narrated by an-Nasaa'i in as-Sunan al-Kubra (8889); classed as Saheeh by al-Albaani in as-Saheehah (315).

BOWING IN SPORTS

Ibn Taymiyah said: "With regard to bowing in greeting, this is forbidden as narrated in al-Tirmidhi from the Prophet ﷺ that they asked him about a man who meets his brother and bows to him, and he said no to that. That is because it is not permitted to bow or prostrate for anyone except Allah."

(Majmoo' al-Fataawa, 1/377).

Question: We joined a karate club in America and the trainer said that you have to bow when he bows to you. We refused and explained to him that this is against our religion, and he accepted that but he said that we should tilt our heads only, because he is the one who bows first and it is essential to return his greeting. What is your opinion on that?

Answer: It is not permissible to bow in greeting to a Muslim or to a Kaafir, whether that involves the upper part of the body or the head, because bowing is a kind of worship, and worship is only for Allah alone.

Fataawa al-Lajnah ad-Daaimah, 1/171.

WRESTLING

There is no harm in practicing freestyle wrestling so long as it does not involve danger, harm, or uncovering one's `Awrah (parts of the body that must be covered in public). The Hadeeth mentions that the Prophet ﷺ wrestled Yazeed ibn Rukaanah and defeated him. This is because the basic ruling expresses permission unless otherwise declared by Islamic law. (Part No. 4; Page No. 411).

As for freestyle wrestling in which wrestlers deem it lawful to hurt one another and cause injury, the council views that it completely resembles boxing even if there are slight differences between them, because the legal physical reasons for the prohibitions of boxing exist in freestyle wrestling that assumes the nature of fighting. Thus, it takes the same ruling of prohibition. Regarding other types of wrestling practiced for physical exercise without causing any injury, they are legally permissible and the council does not view their prohibition. (Part No. 4; Page No. 413).

BOXING

The Academy Council has unanimously agreed that boxing as practiced nowadays in contests and sports centers in our countries is a prohibited practice in the Islamic Sharee`ah. It is based on permitting fighters to injure each other to the extent that could lead to blindness, permanent severe brain damage, serious fractures, or death; without imposing any liability on the other party. In addition, spectators derive pleasure from the winner's victory and feelings of happiness for the injury suffered by the loser. This is absolutely prohibited and rejected in Islam for Allah (Exalted be He) states, ...and do not throw yourselves into destruction And He (Exalted be He) says: And do not kill yourselves (nor kill one another). Surely, Allah is Most Merciful to you. In addition to the statement of the Prophet ﷺ "There is no harm (in Islam) nor should one cause harm (either to himself or to others)". Thus, the jurists of Sharee`ah state that if a person makes his blood violable to another, saying: (kill me), it is impermissible for the other to do this and if he does, he shall be liable to punishment. (Part No. 4; Page No. 412).

The Islamic Fiqh Academy of the Muslim World League in its tenth session held at Makkah Al-Mukarramah during the period (from Sat. Safar 24, 1408 A.H./October 17, 1987 A.D. to Wed. Safar 28, 1408 A.H/Oct. 21, 1987 A.D.)

The Islamic sharee'ah permits all things that are beneficial to the body and do not harm it, and it forbids all things that may cause damage or harm to the body. The Prophet ﷺ said: "Your body has rights over you."

(Al-Bukhaari, Kitaab al-Sawm, 1839).

Boxing is the worst kind of sport, and probably it does not even deserve to be called a sport, despite the fact that western nations, in particular – where boxing is widespread at a professional level – call it "the noble sport" and a form of self-defense. They forget, or overlook, the fact that the main aim of boxing is to harm one's opponent and throw him to the ground, preferably with the "decisive blow" (or "knock-out"), as they call it, which is the highest level of victory in boxing.

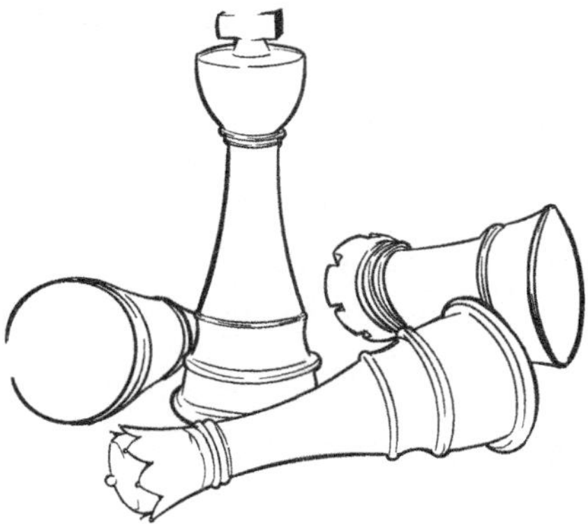

CHESS

What's the Islamic ruling on chess?

Shaykh Al-Albaani:
Chess has no authentic Hadeeth prohibiting it. Only, its situation is like many modern diversions, so if there's no clear violation of Islamic law in it, it's allowed to play it from time to time by way of giving oneself a break, not making it a habit and becoming [avidly] interested in it, because it will lead people [like that] into neglecting many of the obligations that are upon them to stick to and take care of.

But chess, up until today, has an evil that remaining with its pieces: it has some idols like an elephant [in some versions of it], a horse, and the like of that. Because of this, whoever has a chess [set] in his house and wants to engage in it as a diversion—[following] the previously mentioned condition, i.e., [that he only plays it] from time to time—it's an Islamic requirement upon him that he makes changes to these forms and these figures [or idols] and [strike] their heads [off], since the [prohibited] image is the head, as has come in Hadeeth. At that point, it's possible to play with them upon the condition that I mentioned earlier [of playing only from time to time].

And it's been narrated as coming from ʿAli, ﷺ and I, when I say, "it's been narrated," I mean what I say, which is: with a chain of narration that has some weakness in it—that he passed by some people bent over, engrossed in playing chess, so he said to them: "What are these idols that you are keeping yourselves to out of devotion?" *(Al-Anbiyā' 52 extracted.)*

Because the reality of how these players and the onlookers around them were sitting [was that] you see them absorbed, bent over with engrossed interest over the game. So ʿAli pulled out this verse on them, denouncing them. He said: "What are these idols that you are keeping yourselves to out of devotion?"

So, before everything, it's an Islamic requirement to make changes to these figures [by removing their heads]; after that, [it's allowed] if one plays with them from time to time as we've said, without [the game] taking one away from attendance at the mosque [to] pray with the Muslims and without preoccupying one from taking care of one's religious and household obligations, etc.

Fataawa Raabigh, no. 1 (00:35:41), as quoted in Jaamiʿ Al-Turaath Al-Albaani fī Al-Fiqh, vol. 16, p. 414.

BACKGAMMON

It is not permissible to play backgammon because it involves the use of dice which is Haraam and emphatically forbidden.

Buraida reported on the authority of his father that Allah's Apostle ﷺ said: He who played Nardasheer (dice) is like one who dyed his hand with the flesh and blood of swine.

Saheeh Muslim, 2260.

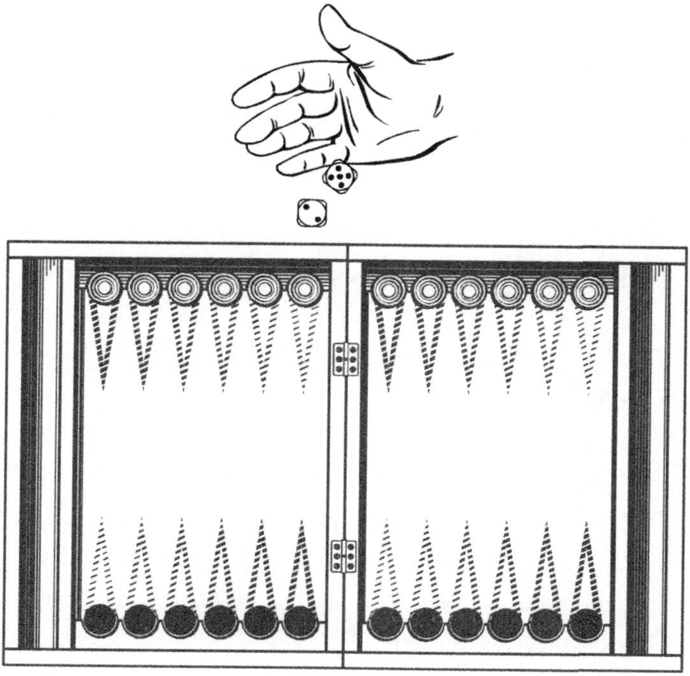

THE RULING ON PLAYING VIDEO GAMES

As a general rule, these games are okay as long as they don't interfere with necessary obligations like establishing prayer (i.e., praying correctly and on time) and honoring one's parents, and as long as they don't contain anything that is Haraam.

There are, however, many Haraam elements in these games, such as the following:

Games which approve and promote witchcraft & sorcery.

Games that include depictions of nudity which corrupt morals.

Music and other things that are known to be forbidden in Islam.

PLAYING CARDS AND OTHER SIMILAR GAMES

Question: Shaykh, we'd like to know the Islamic ruling on some modern games: we call them "carrom," "billiards," and "dominoes." What's the Islamic ruling on playing [these], or, you know, cards…?

Shaykh Al-Albaani:
Yes, these games are without doubt of various kinds. For example, al-shaddah [the deck]—these playing cards—these are without a doubt, a game of the disbelievers, those who worship others along with

Allah, who've represented their beliefs and worship of others along with Allah in some of the pictures they've printed on some of the cards; among them is a young man and among them is a girl, and others along those lines. Playing with these types of cards—and, as you know, the topic of discussion right now is not gambling—but playing with these types of cards as a [form of] recreation or, as you all say, "passing through [literally, "cutting"] time" or "wasting time"—and this is from the ignorance of Muslims today that they don't remember the old Arabic proverb: "Time is like a sword; if you don't cut it [i.e., pass through it actively], it will cut you [i.e., pass through you]"—so this is from the things Muslims are going through today; they waste something whose value is more precious than gold and silver, and that is nothing other than time.

What then serves as evidence [here] is that playing with these cards without gambling is not free, at the very least, [of being considered something detested in Islam] because of what there is in it of using these images [of living, animate beings] and becoming involved and bending over engrossed with interest in playing with them, as is seen from players.

And this reminds me of a report that's been narrated as coming from ʿAli—and I mean what I say when I say, "been narrated," because the [statement] "been narrated" is an indirect way of indicating [that the narration] is considered weak—so it's been narrated from ʿAli, may Allah be pleased with him, that he passed by some people who were playing chess, bending over and deeply engrossed in it, so he said to them: "What are these idols that you are keeping yourselves to out of devotion?"

(Al-Anbiyaa, 52 extracted, English meaning).

So, he pulled out this verse on them, why? Because chess really does have figures [or idols] in it: it has a horse, it has an elephant [in some versions], it has a king, and so on. And these [players] were bending over, completely engrossed in it. So, he used that as proof against them, denouncing this avid interest [of theirs] and [their] bending over [it] with [so much] absorption, even though they weren't, without any doubt, intent on the idols—they were intent on the game and charging up their abilities to memorize or remember things and things like that. But this despicable outer appearance of bending over, engrossed with figures [or idols], it's from this angle that I hold playing with these cards to be something detested [in Islam], due to what's in them of images that represent the disbelief of those who invented these cards.

Then after that, playing with these cards is of different kinds. Some [games] are based on working one's ability to remember or memorize things; some are based on what they call "luck." It's this latter kind that has a similarity to dice, about which the explicit, authentic text has come [to us] in Saheeh Muslim from the Prophet ﷺ, [in which] he said that one who plays with dice is like one who dips his hands into the flesh and blood of pigs.

Similarly, he prohibited in the Hadeeth of Abu Moosa Al-Ashʿari … the Messenger of Allah ﷺ prohibited [the use] of dice. Dice [rolls] are based on luck, and it's because of that you find [among] people playing with them [those who] call out, "[C'mon], dice" … "[C'mon], luck" …. This kind of playing with cards takes the same ruling of dice, which has been forbidden [explicitly] in textual form.

As for those types [of games] that are from the angle of sharpening the memory, the ruling on [those] is the same as the Islamic ruling on chess with an exception [that must be noted] …. So, I'm saying its Islamic ruling is the same as the ruling on chess in view of there being some use of the intellect in it, but we've noted as an exception these figures [of animate beings], and that it's not allowed to become engrossed with them. It's for that reason, we advise those who've sometimes been put to trial by these games to cut off the heads of these small figures so that it becomes allowed to keep them for this game.

And it's in this way this [whole] discussion can take various forms and involve various details; it could take a long time to delve into them. But the guideline to follow is only that any game that has figures [of animate beings]—has images—it's obligatory to stay away from it. As for [those games] that don't have any of that, it's allowed to play with them from time to time, from the angle of giving oneself a break. As for making it a habit, where it takes up all one's time and all one's thoughts, and maybe one forgets one's prayers and worship, and maybe one forgets his wife and children, then at this point, this would be considered like alcohol, which keeps [people] from praying and remembering Allah.

So, becoming occupied with these games from time to time, as a form of recreation or giving oneself a break—there's nothing wrong with that. As to what concerns some [games], as it happens, I don't know their names because I've never heard of them before just now, then if it's enough to answer [the question with something] like a general principle, it's possible for things to become clear [for the one asking] from this [following] description: whichever games have images or forms [of animate beings] in them, it is obligatory to stay away from them, and whichever don't have anything of that in them and aren't games based upon luck, but only upon memory and using the intellect, then it's allowed on the final condition that it does not keep [one] from praying and remembering Allah.

As'ilah wa Fataawa Al-Imaaraatiyyah, no. 5 (00:46:33), as quoted in Jaami' Al-Turaath Al-Albaani fi Al-Fiqh, vol. 16, pp. 418-20.

HOW TO TREAT YOUR PARENTS

Shaykh al-Sa'di said: "be dutiful and kind to parents" means: treat them kindly in all ways, in word and in deed. *(Tafseer al-Sa'di, p. 524)*

Ways to honor your parents

1. Gratitude

Your parents have provided you with more than just food and shelter. Any child could never imagine the sacrifices that each parent makes in terms of sleep, work, career, and lifestyle. Show gratitude to them as a form of reciprocation.

2. Be sensitive towards their feelings

We don't realize it as we get older that they are getting older as well. They become more sensitive, and even the tiniest act of negligence on your part can cause them harm. As a result, be sensitive. Make time for them, sit with them, and have a long conversation with them.

3. Take care of them

They looked after you when you were a baby and were completely reliant on them. Now that they're older, it's up to you to look after them.

4. Obey them

Your parents are looking out for your best interests. Pay attention to their suggestions and follow them. You should only disobey your parents if they give you anti-Islam advice.

5. Respect them

Sometimes it becomes really hard to be patient with your parents. It can be totally exasperating. But hey, don't lose your cool. Speak to them in a polite manner, let them begin the meals, let them walk ahead of you. Little things can make them feel valued and respected.

The Prophet ﷺ said: "The pleasure of Allah is in pleasing one's father and the anger of Allah is in angering one's father."

Narrated by al-Tirmidhi, 1821; classed as Saheeh by Ibn Hibaan and al-Haakim

BEST DUAA FOR YOUR PARENTS

رَّبِّ ارْحَمْهُمَا كَمَا رَبَّيَانِي صَغِيرًا

My Lord, have mercy on them, as they raised me when I was a child.

(Surah Al-Israa 17-24).

رَبَّنَا اغْفِرْ لِي وَلِوَالِدَيَّ وَلِلْمُؤْمِنِينَ يَوْمَ يَقُومُ الْحِسَابُ

Our Lord! Forgive me, my parents, and the believers on the Day when the judgment will come to pass.

(Surah Ibrahim, 14:41).

IMITATING THE KUFFAAR

Ibn Uthaymeen said: "The problem now is that there are some people who think that imitating the Kuffaar is a glory and they think that returning to what the Prophet and his companions were upon is backwardness!"

Kutubun wa rasaailu li-'Uthaymeen (8, p.117)

It was narrated from Abu Sa'eed al-Khudri that the Prophet ﷺ said: "You will certainly follow the ways of those who came before you handspan by handspan, cubit by cubit, to the extent that if they entered the hole of a lizard, you will enter it too." We said: "O Messenger of Allah, (do you mean) the Jews and the Christians?" He said: "Who else?"

Narrated by al-Bukhaari, 1397; Muslim, 4822.

It was narrated that 'Abd-Allah ibn 'Umar said: The Prophet ﷺ said: "Whoever imitates a people is one of them."

Narrated by Abu Dawood, 3512; classed as saheeh by al-Albaani in Irwa' al-Ghaleel, 2691.

Shaykh Al-Albaani said:
"The weak imitate the strong and strong do not imitate the weak"

Those Muslims who imitate the Kuffaar and Fussaaq have an inferiority complex. Be proud of your Islam and be proud of your identity!

GUIDELINE ON THE ISSUE OF IMITATING THE KUFFAAR

Shaykh Muhammad ibn 'Uthaymeen was asked: What is the guideline on the issue of imitating the Kuffaar?

He replied:

Imitation of the Kuffaar may be in appearance, clothing, food, and other things because it is a general word that refers to a person doing something that is done exclusively by the Kuffaar, in such a way that whoever sees him would think that he is one of the Kuffaar. This is the guideline. But if the thing has become widespread among both Muslims and Disbelievers, then this imitation is permissible, even if it was originally taken from the Kuffaar, so long as it is not Haraam in and of itself, such as wearing silk. End quote.

Majmoo' Duroos wa Fataawa al-Haram al-Makki (3/367).

With regard to the phrase "imitation of the kuffaar", that does not mean that we should not use anything that they have manufactured. No one says such a thing. At the time of the Prophet ﷺ and afterwards the people used to wear clothes made by the Kuffaar and use vessels made by them.

Imitation of the Kuffaar means **imitating their clothing and appearance, and the customs that are unique to them.** It does not mean that we should not ride what they ride or wear what they wear. But if they ride in a specific way that is unique to them, then we should not ride in that way. If they tailor their clothes in a certain fashion that is unique to them, we should not do likewise. But if we have cars that are similar to theirs and fabric that is similar to theirs, there is nothing wrong with that.

Majmoo' Fataawa al-Shaykh Ibn 'Uthaymeen, 12, question 177.

DISCRIMINATION IN PUNISHMENT

Discrimination in punishments, penalties, and regulations between the weak and the upper class was one of the ways of the **Jews**. In the two Saheehs is the story of Usaamah Bin Zaid's intercession on behalf of a woman who stole. The Prophet ﷺ said to him, "O Usaamah, you intercede concerning one of Allah's limits - the children of Israel were destroyed because they used to intercede. That is, if one of their upper class stole they would leave him alone, and if the poor stole they implemented their punishment on him. I swear by He whose Hand my soul is in that if Fatimah the daughter of Muhammad stole, I would cut off her hand."

LONG NAILS

Shaykh Abd al-Azeez Ibn Baaz said:
Elongation of the (toe and finger) nails is in opposition to the Sunnah. It also comprises imitating some animals and the disbelievers.

Majmoo Al-Fataawa (49/10)

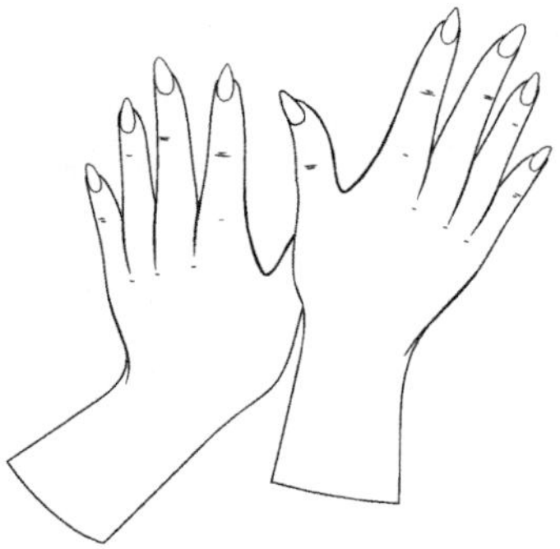

Females with Long Nails:
It's a symbol of ignorance. If she has (fake) super long nails, she's cursed with cerebral inferiority. She wasn't brought up to value reason and logic over emotion and whim. Instead, she values superficiality over meaningfulness. Her parents didn't discipline and guide her to think for herself; she needs media and mass to do her thinking for her, telling her what matters or not, what is beautiful or not. And yes, it's unhygienic, uncomfortable, and unpragmatic.

EXCESSIVE LOVE FOR DOGS

Islam does not enjoin anything but that which is good for people, and it does not forbid them anything but that which is harmful to them. The Prophet ﷺ enjoined washing vessels that have been licked by a dog, and that is only because its **saliva is impure**.

Shaykh Ibn 'Uthaymeen said:
"With regard to touching the dog, if there is no wetness then it does not make the hand Najis (impure), but if he touches it and there is any wetness, then this means that the hand becomes Najis (impure) according to the view of many scholars, and the hand must be washed after those seven times, one of which should be with soil."

Majmu' Fataawa Ibn 'Uthaymeen, 11/246

It was narrated from Abu Hurayrah that the Messenger of Allah ﷺ said: "The purification of the vessel of one of you, if a dog licks it, is to wash it seven times, the first time with soil." *Narrated by Muslim, 279.*

And according to another report by *Muslim (280):* "If a dog licks the vessel of one of you, let him wash it seven times and rub it with soil the eighth time."

According to a report narrated by Abu Dawood (68) from Kabshah bint Ka'b ibn Maalik: Abu Qutaadah entered and she poured some water for him to do wudoo'. A cat came and drank from the water, and he tipped the vessel for it so that it could drink. Kabshah said: "He saw me looking at him and he said, 'Do you find it strange, O daughter of my brother?' I said, 'Yes.' He said, 'The Messenger of Allah ﷺ said, "They (cats) are not Najis (impure), rather they are among those who go around among you (al-tawwaafeena 'alaykum)."

These two reports were classed as saheeh by al-Bukhaari, al-Daaraqutni and others, as was stated in al-Talkhees by Ibn Hajar, 1/15.

So, based on the above narrations and proofs it is clear that dogs are not equal to cats when it comes to purity, yet we see many Muslims today who hug, kiss, get licked by dogs and are fine with it. This is because either they were raised in the western society and can't get over their excessive love and obsession for dogs or Muslims who think that imitating the western culture is a glory.

Is it really humanitarian?
There is a strong sentimentalization of dogs instilled in western culture from an early age. Bookshops/Internet sites have shelves/pages full of children's books where the characters are dogs. We all have met people who

sleep with their dogs, buy expensive beds & accessories for them, but put their parents in old people's homes!

Dogs as pets

Raising or keeping a dog inside the house is not allowed in Islam under any circumstances, and even prevents the Angels of Mercy from entering the house, and deducts a large amount of a Muslim's worship reward on every single day.

Dogs are only allowed to be kept for a few reasons: to guard wealth, farmland and property, and as a sheepdog, or for herding and for hunting—added to that is what some scholars have allowed: police sniffer dogs for explosives, narcotics, etc. (Fatwa of *Al-Lajnah Ad-Dā'imah*, 4/195). And also, to protect the homes of people if there is a need for that—due to them being isolated and vulnerable, as stated by Shaykh Ibn 'Uthaymeen and alluded to by Ibn Abdil-Barr (in *At-Tamheed*), and Allah knows best. **As for keeping them as pets or companions, then that is not allowed.**

Abu Hurayrah narrated that the Prophet ﷺ said: "Whoever keeps a dog, except a dog for herding, hunting or farming, one Qiraat will be deducted from his reward each day."

Narrated by Muslim, 1575.

Al-Nawawi said:

"There is a difference of opinion as to whether it is permissible to keep dogs for purposes other than these three, such as for guarding houses and roads. The most correct view is that it is permissible, by analogy with these three and based on the reason that is to be understood from the hadeeth, which is necessity."

(Sharh Muslim, 10/236)

Shaykh Ibn 'Uthaymeen said:
"Based on this, if a house is in the middle of the city there is no need to keep a dog to guard it, so keeping a dog for this purpose in such situations is Haraam and is not permitted, and it detracts one or two Qiraats from a person's reward every day. They should get rid of this dog and not keep it. But if the house is in the countryside and there is no one else around, then it is permissible to keep a dog to guard the house and the people who are in it; guarding the members of the household is more important than guarding livestock or crops."

(Majmu' Fataawa Ibn 'Uthaymeen, 4/246).

EYEBROW SHAPING & PLUCKING

Hair which we are forbidden to remove, which includes the eyebrows. The action of removing the hair of the eyebrows is called al-nams. It is also forbidden to remove the hair of the beard.

The evidence for that is the hadeeth of 'Abd-Allah ibn Mas'ood who said: I heard the Messenger of Allah ﷺ

say: "Allah has cursed the woman who does tattoos and the one who has them done, the woman who plucks eyebrows (al-namisah) and the one who has it done (al-mutanammisah), and the one who files her teeth for the purpose of beauty, altering the creation of Allah."

(Narrated by al-Bukhaari, 5931; Muslim, 2125)

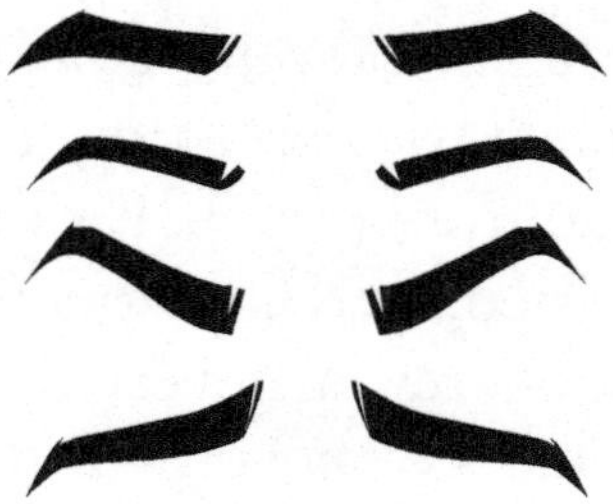

"Al-Nams means plucking the hair of the eyebrows, which is not permissible because the Prophet ﷺ cursed the woman who plucks eyebrows (al-namisah) and the one who has it done (al-mutanammisah)."

(Fataawa al-Lajnah al-Daaimah, 5/195)

LOWERING THE GAZE

Lowering the gaze (ghadd al-basr) means restraining the gaze and not allowing it to wander or dwell upon anything.

Ibn al-Qayyim said:
Looking generates thoughts, then thoughts generate ideas, then ideas generate desire, then desires generate will, then the will grows strong and resolves to do the deed, and then the deed will inevitably take place unless there is something to prevent it. Concerning this, it was said that patience in lowering the gaze is easier than patience in bearing the pain that comes afterward. End quote.

Al-Jawaab al-Kaafi (p. 106).

The Prophet ﷺ said:
"There is not a man who is alone with a woman except that Shaytaan is the third amongst them."

Reported by at-Tirmidhi, no. 2165; an-Nasā'i in al-Kubraa, no. 9219.

This hadeeth proves that the origin of the affair is that it is forbidden to look at strange or unrelated women – and that is because the Prophet ﷺ only made the allowance for the one proposing marriage. So, this proves that the origin is that it is prohibited due to the tribulations and temptations it leads to. Allah, the Most High, said: "Tell the believing men to lower their gazes and guard their private parts. That is purer for them. Indeed, Allah is Acquainted with what they do. And tell

the believing women to lower their gazes and guard their private parts."
[Surah An-Noor 30-31]

THREE EYES WILL NEVER ENTER THE HELLFIRE

Abu Rayhanah reported: The Messenger of Allah ﷺ said, "The Hellfire is forbidden for the eye weeping from the fear of Allah. The Hellfire is forbidden for the eye vigilant in the way of Allah. The Hellfire is forbidden for the eye that lowers its gaze from what Allah has forbidden."

Source: al-Sunan al-Kubraa lil-Nasaa'i, 8818.
Grade: Hasan li ghayrihi (fair due to external evidence) according to Al-Albaani

ALLAH KNOWS WHICH MEN GAZE AT WOMEN OR NOT

Ibn Abbas reported: A woman would pray behind the Messenger of Allah ﷺ, who was the most beautiful of all people. Some men would come early to be in the first row, so as not to gaze at her. Some of them would come late to be in the last row. When they bowed, they would look at her between their limbs. Allah Almighty revealed the verse, "We surely know who comes first among you and We surely know who comes last." (15:24)

Source: Sunan al-Tirmidhii 3122, Grade: Sahih (authentic) according to Al-Albaani

WHO IS WEAKER THAN A MAN UNABLE TC LOWER HIS GAZE?

Abu Nu'aym reported: Sufyan al-Thawri, may Allal have mercy on him, said, "A woman will pass by a mar and he cannot restrain himself from looking at he lustfully although there is no benefit in it. What coulc be weaker than this?"

Source: Hilyat al-Awliyaa' 7/68

MEN MUST RESPECT WOMEN, NOT STARI AT THEM

Ibn Abbas reported: Al-Fadl was riding with th Messenger of Allah ﷺ and a woman from Khash'an came. Al-Fadl began to stare at her and she stared a him. The Prophet made Al-Fadl turn his face in th other direction.

Source: Saheeh Al-Bukhaari 1442, Saheeh Muslim 1334.
Grade: Muttafaqun Alayhi (authenticity agreed upon) according to Al-Bukhaari an Muslim

DO NOT TAKE A SECOND GLANCE AT A WOMAN

Buraydah reported: The Messenger of Allah ﷺ said "Do not follow one glance at a woman with another Verily, you have the first one and not the second."

Source: Sunan al-Tirmidhī 2777
Grade: Hasan (fair) according to Al-Albaani.

The words do not follow a glance with another mean do not look again after the first glance. You will be forgiven for the first means that you will be forgiven if the first glance was unintentional, and but not for the second means that because the second glance was by choice, it will be counted against you.

ACCIDENTALLY GLANCING AT A WOMAN

Jareer reported: I asked the Messenger of Allah ﷺ about accidentally glancing at a woman. The Prophet ordered me to look the other way.

Source: Saheeh Muslim 2159.
Grade: Saheeh (authentic) according to Muslim

MANNERS & CHARACTER

Narrated Abu Hurayrah:
The Prophet ﷺ said: The most perfect believer in respect of faith is he who is best of them in manners.

Sunan Abi Dawud 4682, Grade: Hasan Saheeh (Al-Albaani).

The best Muslims, first and foremost, are those who have the best character. The term 'character' has a broad meaning in this context, encompassing good behavior toward Allah, other people, and society as a whole. All of the Islamic virtues, such as justice, compassion, humility, and truthfulness, are included.

Good character towards people can be summarized as treating others the way you would love to be treated and being a good neighbor.

YOUR IMPRESSION OF OTHERS

Deception, lying, cheating, or manipulation should not be practiced by Muslims in general or by people of knowledge in particular, as this will cause the people to turn away from hearing the truth. This could be as a result of your interactions (with others), bad character, or deceitful business transactions. It may become known that you are deceitful, misleading, and delusory, or that you have bad manners and are untrustworthy in your dealings (with others).

So, beware, Muslim youth, of becoming a person of bad character in your treatment of others, including (treatment of) your immediate or extended families, as well as your dealings with people in general. Be cautious of having the trait of duplicity (fraudulence), as well as other negative qualities and a repulsive personality.

Muslim youth must possess the best qualities and temperament in terms of character, interactions, and overall disposition.

MISUSE OF INSHA'ALLAH

Al-Awzaa'e said:
To make a promise saying: Insha'Allah, whilst having the intention of not fulfilling it is **hypocrisy.**

Jaami Al-Uloom wal-Hikam 2/482

A List of General Manners for Every Muslim

1. TAKE CARE OF GUESTS

Abu Shuraih reported: The Messenger of Allah ﷺ said, "Whoever believes in Allah and the Last Day, let him honor his guest and recompense him." They said, "O Messenger of Allah, what is his recompense?" The Prophet said, "It is for a day and a night, as good hospitality is for three days and after that it is charity." And the Prophet said, "Whoever believes in Allah and the Last Day, let him speak goodness or remain silent."

Source: Saheeh Al-Bukhaari 5673, Sahih Muslim 3255
Grade: Muttafaqun Alayhi (authenticity agreed upon) according to Al-Bukhaari and Muslim

2. BE JUST, EVEN AGAINST YOURSELF

We must always stand for justice in Islam, whether for Muslims or non-Muslims, even if justice is against us.

Allah said:
O you who believe, be persistently standing firm in justice as witnesses for Allah, even if it be against yourselves or parents and relatives. Whether one is rich or poor, Allah is more worthy of both. Follow not your desires, lest you not be just. If you distort your testimony or refuse to give it, then Allah is aware of what you do.

Surah An-Nisaa 4:135

3. DO NOT ACCUSE OTHERS OF IMMORALITY WITHOUT PROOF

Abu Dharr reported: The Prophet ﷺ said, "A man does not accuse another man of wickedness or unbelief but that it will be turned against him, if his companion is innocent."

Source: Saheeh Al-Bukhaari 6045
Grade: Sahih (authentic) according to Al-Bukhaari

4. AVOID ASKING TOO MANY FAVORS FROM OTHERS

Al-Bukhaari (1469) and Muslim (1053) narrated from Abu Sa'eed al-Khudri that some people from among the Ansaar asked the Messenger of Allah ﷺ and he gave them, then they asked him and he gave them, then they asked him and he gave them, until what he had was exhausted. He said: "Whatever I have of good I will never withhold from you, but whoever refrains from asking (of people), Allah will make him content whoever seeks to be independent of means, Allah will make him independent, and whoever strives to be patient Allah will bestow patience upon him, and no one is ever given anything better and more abundant than patience."

An-Nawawi said:
In this hadeeth we are encouraged to refrain from asking of people and to be content with what is available, so as to preserve one's dignity, even if what is available is little.

End quote from Sharh Muslim (7/126)

5. AVOID ASKING UNNECESSARY QUESTIONS

Shaykh as-Sa'di said in his commentary on the verse in al-Maa'idah: Allah forbids His believing slaves to ask about things which, if they are made plain to them, will cause them trouble and grief, such as when some of the Muslims asked the Messenger of Allah ﷺ about their fathers, or about their situation in Paradise or Hell. Perhaps if these matters were made plain to the one who asked, there would be nothing good for him in it. Another example is when they asked about things that had not happened, or they asked about things that would lead to stricter rulings in sharee'ah that could cause hardship for the ummah, or they asked about matters that do not concern them. Asking about these and similar matters is what is forbidden. As for asking questions that will not result in any such thing, this is what is enjoined, as Allah, may He be exalted, says (interpretation of the meaning):

"So ask those who possess knowledge if you do not know" *[Surah an-Nahl 16:43]*.

6. DO NOT BE MISERLY NOR EXTRAVAGANT

MISERLINESS

Ibn al-Qayyim said:

The miserly person is the one who withholds what he is required to give. The one who gives all that he is obliged to give cannot be called miserly; rather the miserly person is the one who withholds what is due from him to give.

End quote from Jalaa' al-Afhaam (p. 385).

Shaykh Ibn 'Uthaymeen said something similar: Miserliness is withholding what is obligatory and what should be given.

End quote from Sharh Riyaadh as-Saaliheen (3/410).

<u>EXTRAVAGANCE</u>

Shaykh Ibn 'Uthaymeen also said:
Excess or extravagance means overstepping the mark, and Allah, may He be exalted, has stated in His Book that He does not love those who commit excess. If we say that excess or extravagance means overstepping the mark, then excess varies. This thing may be extravagant in the case of one person, and not extravagant in the case of another. One person may buy a house costing two million riyals, and furnish it for six hundred thousand, and buy a car; if he is rich, then he is not committing excess, because these things are easily affordable for those who are very rich. But if he is not rich, then he is regarded as committing excess, whether he is one of the middle class or among the poor, because some poor people want to project an image of wealth, so you see them buying big houses and furnishing them with expensive furnishings, and they may have borrowed some of that from people. This is wrong.

So, there are three categories, the first of which is one who is very wealthy. In this case, we say that at the present time – and we do not say that this is applicable in all times – if he buys a house for two million riyals, and furnishes it for six hundred thousand riyals, and buys a car, then he is not committing excess.

The second category is the middle class; in this case, such purchases are regarded as committing excess.

The third category is the poor; in the case of a poor man, such purchases are regarded as foolishness, for how can he borrow money in order to project an image for which he has no need?!

End quote.

Liqa' al-Baab al-Maftooh (107/23).

7. STRICLY AVOID DECEPTION IN BUSINESS OR TRADE

The Deceptive Sale

It is when you deceive your Muslim brother by selling him a product that has defects and you know about these defects yet you do not inform him about them. So, this kind of sale is not permissible and it is from deception, swindling and fraud.

It is obligatory on the seller to make these defects clear to the seller and to let him know about them. But if he fails to inform him about them, then this is from deception and swindling.

One time the Messenger of Allah ﷺ passed by a person selling some food in the marketplace who had his food in a pile. So, the Prophet ﷺ put his noble hand inside the pile of food and found some wet portions in the bottom of the pile. So, he said: "What is this O owner of the food?" He said: "The sky has affected it" – meaning the rain has damaged some of it. So, Allah's Messenger ﷺ said: "Then won't you make it visible so that the people can see it? Whoever cheats us (i.e. swindles Muslims) is not from us."

This hadeeth is considered one of the fundamental principles in conducting business transactions between the Muslims. So, it is not permissible for a Muslim to conceal the defects. If his merchandise has a defect then he must make it visible so that the buyer sees it and is aware of it, and so that he could acquire the item for a price that is appropriate for this defect. He must not acquire the item for the price it would be if it were flawless, for then the seller would be deceiving, cheating, fooling and swindling, based on the saying of Allah's Messenger: "Then won't you make it visible so that the people can see it? Whoever cheats us is not from us."

"Forbidden Business Transactions in Islam" by Shaykh Saaleh Al-Fawzaan

"Changing the definition and name of things that are Haraam when their essence remains the same is even more evil, as well as involving an attempt to deceive Allah and His Messenger, and claiming that Islam accepts trickery, deception, cheating and hypocrisy, and that sharee'ah forbids something because it is evil but then allows it when it becomes even worse. Hence

Ayyoob al-Sakhtiyaani said that some people try to cheat Allah like they cheat children. If they were to commit the sin believing that it is a sin that would be less serious." *Ighaathat al-Lahfaan, 1/354.*

8. DON'T ENTER HOMES WITHOUT PERMISSION

Allah, may He be exalted, says:

"O you who believe! Enter not houses other than your own, until you have asked permission and greeted those in them; that is better for you, in order that you may remember" *[Surah an-Noor 24:27]*

The Prophet ﷺ said: It is not permissible for a Muslim to look inside any house until he has been given permission."

Al-Bukhaari in al-Adab al-Mufrad (1093); classed as saheeh by al-Albaani.

The requirement to seek permission to enter has been enjoined so as to prevent looking, as the Prophet ﷺ said: Seeking permission is enjoined only so as to prevent looking." *Narrated by al-Bukhaari (6241).*

One should not seek permission to enter aggressively, or bang on the door or ring the bell aggressively, because that is rude and is not polite. It was narrated that Anas ibn Maalik said: People used to knock on the doors of the Prophet ﷺ with their fingernails.

Narrated by al-Bukhaari in al-Adab al-Mufrad (1080). Classed as saheeh by al-Albaani.

One should seek permission to enter three times, unless he is certain or thinks it most likely that the people inside the house did not hear him. The Prophet ﷺ said "If one of you seeks permission to enter three times but is not given permission, let him go back." *Narrated by al-Bukhaari (6245).*

It is Sunnah not to stand facing the door, so that one's gaze will not fall upon anything inside the house. Rather one should stand to one side of the door, either on the right or left. It was narrated from Talhah that Huzay said: A man came and stood at the door of the Prophet ﷺ asking permission to enter, and he stood at the door – 'Uthmaan said: facing the door. The Prophet ﷺ said "(Stand) like this or like this (i.e., to one side or other of the door), for seeking permission is enjoined only so as to prevent looking."

Narrated by Abu Dawood (5174); classed as saheeh by al-Albaani. It says in 'Awn al-Ma'bood: That is, he should step away from the door, and face some other direction.

9. DO NOT INSULT OTHERS

Allah, may He be exalted, says (interpretation of the meaning): And do not insult one another and do not call each other by [offensive] nicknames. *[al-Hujuraat 49:11]*

The Messenger of Allah ﷺ said, "The believer does not insult others, does not curse others, is not vulgar, and is not shameless."

(Sunan al-Tirmidhi 1977, Classed as saheeh by al-Albaani.

Abu Huraira reported: A man reviled Abu Bakr while the Prophet ﷺ was sitting. Then Abu Bakr reviled the man with the same words and the Prophet became angry and he stood to leave. Abu Bakr went to the Prophet and he said, "O Messenger of Allah, the man reviled me and you were sitting, but when I responded you became angry and stood up." The Prophet said: Verily, there was an angel with you responding on your behalf, but Shaytaan appeared when you responded with the same words as him and I will not sit in the presence of Shaytaan.

Musnad Aḥmad 9411, Grade: Jayyid

10. LYING AND ITS EFFECTS

"There was no behavior more hated to the Messenger of Allah ﷺ than lying."

Narrated by Aaisha, Silsilah Ahadeeth as-Saheehah of Al-Albaani #2052

PRANKS

It is not allowed to scare or frighten another Muslim. Most of the pranks that have been done by people are about scaring, frightening or shocking others. Not to mention the risks associated with such behavior.

Narrated from Abdurrahman ibn Abi Layla, he said: The companions of Muhammad ﷺ narrated to us: They were travelling with the Prophet ﷺ and a man among them fell asleep. Some of them took a rope he had with him, and this frightened him.

The Messenger of Allah ﷺ said:
"It is not permissible for a Muslim to frighten another Muslim".

Saheeh Sunan Abi Dawud 5004.

Lying is one of the characteristics of the hypocrites, and it is a blameworthy trait which encourages one to commit evil and prevents one from doing good.

Narrated by Ibn Mas'ood: The Messenger of Allah ﷺ said: "I enjoin you to be truthful, for truthfulness leads to righteousness and righteousness leads to Paradise. A man may continue to tell the truth and endeavor to be truthful until he is recorded with Allah as a speaker of truth. And beware of lying, for lying leads to wickedness and wickedness leads to Hell. A man may continue to tell lies and endeavor to tell lies, until he is recorded with Allah as a liar."

Al-Bukhaari, 6094 and Muslim, 2607.

Abu Huraira reported: The Messenger of Allah ﷺ said, "Among the signs of a hypocrite are three, even if he fasts and prays and claims to be a Muslim: **when he speaks, he lies,** when he gives a promise, he breaks it, and when he is trusted, he betrays."

Al-Bukhaari, 33 and Muslim, 59

Grade: Muttafaqun Alayhi (authenticity agreed upon) according to Al-Bukhaari and Muslim

11. SPREADING FAKE NEWS

Even if the information is positive, everyone should double-check the facts before passing them along to ensure that they are accurate, in case the individual who passed the information along turns out to be mistaken.

Abu Hurairah said:
The Prophet ﷺ said, "It is enough for a man to prove himself a liar when he goes on narrating whatever he hears."

Saheeh Muslim, Book 17, Hadeeth 37

12. DO NOT REMIND OTHERS OF YOUR FAVORS

It stirs bitter feelings. Invalidates or may even nullify good deeds totally.

Al-Qurtubi said that reminding others of one's favors for them is usually done by a miserly and conceited person. The miser always feels that what he gives is great, even if it is something insignificant. Also, the conceited person tends to glorify himself and feels that he is doing others a great favor by giving to them. The reasons for all this are ignorance and forgetfulness of the favors of Allah. If these people had thought carefully, they would have realized that the taker is the one who does them a favor because of the reward that they obtain for giving to him.

Abu Dharr reported: The Prophet ﷺ said, "There are three to whom Allah will not speak on the Day of

Resurrection: one who does not give anything unless his generosity is praised, a hypocrite who sells goods upon a false oath, and one who trails his garment in pride."

Saheeh Muslim, 106

Narrated by Ibn 'Umar that the Prophet ﷺ said: "Allah will not look at three types of people on the Day of Judgment: the one who is undutiful to his parents, the woman who imitates men and the Dayyooth [the man who approves of the indecency of his womenfolk and who is void of jealousy]. Moreover, three types of people will not enter Paradise: the one who is undutiful to his parents, the one who is addicted to alcohol and the one who reminds others of his favors for them."

An-Nasaa'i, Al-Albaani graded as Saheeh

It was narrated from 'Abdullah bin 'Amr that:
The Prophet ﷺ said: "No one who reminds others of his favors, no one who is disobedient to his parents and no drunkard, will enter Paradise."

Sunan an-Nasa'i 5672, Book 51, Hadeeth 134, Grade: Hasan

13. DO NOT SPREAD GOSSIP

A Muslim is not allowed to backbite, engage in rumors, or spread gossip about another person. Islam teaches its followers to verify their information and refrain from speculation. Slandering, fabricating information to harm another person, and disseminating false rumors are all strictly prohibited.

It is reported that news reached Prophet's companion Hudhaifah that a certain man carried tales. Upon this he remarked: I heard Allah's Messenger ﷺ saying: The malicious tale carrier will not enter Paradise.

Saheeh Muslim, 105.

Abdur Rahman ibn Ghanm reported: The Prophet ﷺ said, "The best servants of Allah are those who remind you of Allah when they are seen. The worst servants of Allah are those who carry gossip, separating between loved ones and seeking misery for the innocent."

Musnad Aḥmad 17998.

14. DO NOT SPY ON ONE ANOTHER

Imaam Al-Nawawi said: Some of the scholars said that Tahassus, 'snooping' means listening to other people's conversations, and Tajassus, 'spying' means seeking out other people's faults. It was also suggested that Tajassus means looking for secrets. The word is mostly used in the sense of evil. The Jaasoos 'spy' is the one who seeks out secrets for evil purposes and the Naamoos is the one who seeks out secrets for good purposes. And it was suggested that Tajassus refers to looking for information for someone else, and Tahassus means looking for information for oneself. This was the view of Tha'lab. And it was said that they mean one and the same, which is seeking out information about people's state of affairs.

It is also narrated in al-Saheehayn from Abu Hurayrah that the Prophet ﷺ said: 'Beware of suspicion, for suspicion is the falsest of speech. Do not eavesdrop; do not spy on one another; do not envy one another; do not forsake one another; do not hate one another. Be, O slaves of Allah, brothers."

Al-Bukhaari, 5144; Muslim, 2563.

Narrated Ibn `Abbas:
The Prophet ﷺ said, "Whoever claims to have seen a dream which he did not see, will be ordered to make a knot between two barley grains which he will not be able to do; **and if somebody listens to the talk of some people who do not like him (to listen) or they run away from him, then molten lead will be**

poured into his ears on the Day of Resurrection; and whoever makes a picture, will be punished on the Day of Resurrection and will be ordered to put a soul in that picture, which he will not be able to do." Ibn `Abbas also narrated a similar hadeeth.

Al-Bukhaari 7042.

15. FORGIVE OTHERS, AS YOU WOULD LIKE ALLAH TO FORGIVE YOU

One of the greatest means that will help the Muslim to free his heart of grudges and rancor is to be keen to show sincerity towards the Muslims in general, and to do that for the sake of Allah, because he knows that Allah is pleased with that and loves it.

When the Messenger of Allah ﷺ was asked, Which of the people is best, he said: "Everyone who is pure of heart and sincere of speech." They said: Sincere of speech, we know what this is, but what is pure of heart? He said: "It is (the heart) that is pious and pure, with no sin, injustice, rancor or envy in it."

Narrated by Ibn Maajah (4216); classed as Saheeh by al-Albaani in Saheeh Ibn Maajah.

Abdullah ibn Amr reported: The Prophet ﷺ said, "Be merciful to others and you will receive mercy. Forgive others and Allah will forgive you."

Musnad Aḥmad 6541, Grade: Saheeh

16. KEEP YOUR TRUSTS & PROMISES

Narrated Abu Hurayra: The Prophet ﷺ said, "The signs of a hypocrite are three:

1. Whenever he speaks, he tells a lie.
2. Whenever he promises, he breaks it (his promise).
3. If you trust him, he proves to be dishonest. (If you keep something as a trust with him, he will not return it.)"

Al-Bukhaari, 33.

'Ubaadah ibn al-Saamit reported: The Messenger of Allah ﷺ said: Guarantee for me six deeds and I will guarantee for you Paradise: Be truthful when you speak, ***keep your promises when you make them***, fulfill the trust when you are trusted, guard your chastity, lower your gaze, and restrain your hands from harming others.

Musnad Aḥmad 22251, Grade: Saheeh

Abdullah ibn Amr reported: The Messenger of Allah ﷺ said: There are four signs that make someone a pure hypocrite and whoever has them has a characteristic of hypocrisy until he abandons it: when he speaks he lies, when he makes a covenant he is treacherous, when he makes a promise he breaks it, and when he argues he is wicked.

Saheeh al-Bukhaari, 34

17. RESTRAIN YOUR ANGER

Anger has numerous detrimental repercussions, but in general, they hurt both the person who is angry and others around them. An angry person may use derogatory language and profanity; he may also physically attack others without restraint, even to the point of murdering.

Abu Hurayrah reported that a man said to the Prophet ﷺ "Advise me." He said, "Do not become angry." The man repeated his request several times, and each time the Prophet ﷺ told him, "Do not become angry."

Al-Bukhaari, Fath al-Baari, 10/456

Anas reported that the Prophet ﷺ passed by some people who were wrestling. He asked, "What is this?" They said: "So-and-so is the strongest, he can beat anybody." The Prophet ﷺ said, "Shall I not tell you who is even stronger than him? The man who, when he is mistreated by another, controls his anger, has defeated his own Shaytaan and the Shaytaan of the one who made him angry."

(Reported by al-Bazzaar, and Ibn Hijr said its isnaad is saheeh. Al-Fath, 10/519)

PURIFICATION

MAJOR & MINOR IMPURITY

Minor impurity is that which necessitates wudoo' but not ghusl, such as the emission of urine, stools and wind from the back passage, eating camel meat, and sleeping.

As for major impurity, it is that which necessitates ghusl, such as intercourse and ejaculation as the result of desire, as in the case of a wet dream or otherwise, or menses or postpartum bleeding.

Fataawa al-Lajnah al-Daa'imah, vol. 3, 4/112.

MOST OF THE PUNISHMENT OF THE GRAVE WILL BE BECAUSE OF URINE

Abu Bakrah reported: The Prophet ﷺ passed by two graves and he said, "Verily, they are both being punished, but not for a sin difficult to avoid. As for one, he is punished for the habit of soiling himself with urine. As for the other, he is punished for the habit of backbiting."

Source: Sunan Ibn Maajah 349, Grade: Saheeh (authentic) according to Al-Albaani

IS IT HARAAM TO URINATE WHILE STANDING?

It is not Haraam for a person to urinate while standing, because it has been authentically reported by al-Bukhaari and Muslim, on the authority of Hudhaifah, that the Prophet ﷺ came to the rubbish pit of a people and urinated while standing.

Al-Bukhaari no.226

Permission to urinate standing has also been narrated from Umar, Ali, ibn Umar and Zaid bin Thaabit, may Allah be pleased with them, due to the above mentioned Hadeeth.

But it is prescribed by the Sunnah for a person to urinate sitting, according to the words of A'ishah, may Allah be pleased with her, who said: 'Whoever told you that the Prophet ﷺ urinated standing, do not believe him. He did not urinate except sitting.'

(At-Tirmidhi no.12 and an-Nisaa'i no. 29)

at-Tirmidhi said: 'This is the best and most correct saying in this matter – also because it is better to guard and protect him from being splashed with his own urine.'

RECITATION & MEMORIZATION

One must have the skills in learning to read the Qur'aan effectively so that they can know the Arabic alphabet well, pronounce it correctly, understand the elocution of reading, and understand its meaning well.

Narrated Aisha:
The Prophet ﷺ said, "Such a person as recites the Qur'aan and masters it by heart, will be with the noble righteous scribes (in Heaven). And such a person exerts himself to learn the Qur'aan by heart, and recites it with great difficulty, will have a double reward."

Al-Bukhaari, 4937.

Narrated from 'Abd-Allah ibn 'Amr that the Prophet ﷺ said: "It will be said to the companion of the Qur'aan: Recite and rise in status, recite as you used to recite in the world, for your status will be at the last verse that you recite."

This hadeeth was classed as saheeh by al-Albaani in al-Silsilah al-Saheehah, 5/218, no. 2240

RESPECT YOUR ELDERS

The Prophet ﷺ said: "He is not one of us who does not show mercy to our young ones and respect our old ones."

Narrated by al-Tirmidhi, 1919; classed as hasan by al-Albaani in Saheeh al-Tirmidhi, 1565.

Honoring the old Muslim by treating him with respect, gentleness, and compassion. By doing so, one is glorifying Allah, because the elders have a special status in the sight of Allah.

The Prophet ﷺ said: "Part of glorifying Allah is honoring the grey-haired Muslim."

Narrated by Abu Dawood, 4843; classed as hasan by al-Albaani.

Not Speaking in Front of Elders

Samurah ibn Jundub said: I was young during the time of Allah's Messenger ﷺ and I had memorized things he had said; nothing stopped me from speaking except for the fact that there were amongst us men who were older than me.

Saheeh Muslim, Kitaab Al-Janaa'iz #964.

And it is reported that Abdullaah bin Al-Mubaarak was once asked about an issue in the presence of Sufyaan ibn Uyainah, so he replied, "We have been forbidden from speaking in front of our seniors."

Al-Dhahabee, Siyar A'laam Al-Nubalaa 8:420.

SALAAH

A FEW COMMON MISTAKES RELATED TO THE SALAAH

Raising the eyes to the sky during Salaah or looking to the right and left without due cause.

Narrated Anas bin Maalik: The Prophet said, "What is wrong with those people who look towards the sky during the prayer?" His talk grew stern while delivering this speech and he said, "They should stop (looking towards the sky during the prayer); otherwise, their eye-sight would be taken away."

Al-Bukhaari, Volume 1, Book 12, Number 717

Narrated Aisha: I asked Allah's Apostle about looking here and there in prayer. He replied, "It is a way of stealing by which Shaytaan takes away (a portion) from the prayer of a person."

Al-Bukhaari, Volume 1, Book 12, Number 718

UNCOVERING SHOULDERS WHILE PRAYING

Question: I would like to inform your eminence that there are many brothers – may Allah guide them – who pray Salaah whilst wearing a single garment below the stomach. As for the garment which is worn on the upper body, they place it on the floor or tie it around their stomach. I hope to convey [your answer to them]. Is their Salaah valid whilst they are exposing their back and stomach? This is repeated often. I hope I will find clarification regarding this, may Allah reward you with goodness.

Response: The obligation upon a believer is to pray whilst wearing a lower garment and an upper garment, and making sure his shoulders – or at least one of them – are covered. If a person wants to pray, he must ensure the upper garment is covering his shoulders, or he wears a shirt if he is not in a state of Ihraam.

Majmoo Fataawa wa Maqaalaat ash-Shaykh Ibn Baaz, Vol 29 Page 217.

PRAYING IN SHORTS

What is required of the worshipper is to cover his Awrah whilst praying, according to the consensus of the Muslims. The Awrah of a man is the area between the navel and the knees, according to the majority of scholars.

Al-Mughni, 3/7; al-Istidhkaar, 2/197; Fataawa Islamiyyah, 1/427

Shaykh Ibn 'Uthaymeen said:
There are several opinions concerning the matter:
One is that the knee is included in the Awrah so it must be covered. The second opinion is that the navel and the knee are both part of the Awrah so they must both be covered. The third opinion – which is the well-known view among our madhhab – is that the navel and the knee are not included in the Awrah, so they do not have to be covered. This is based on the definition of the Awrah as being "between the navel and the knee."

Ash-Sharh al-Mumti', 2/160

Ibn Qudaamah wrote:
"It is sufficient for the Muslim man to cover the area from the **navel** to the **knees** in terms of clearing himself of his liability from the obligation of covering the Awrah during the prayer. In brief, covering the Awrah with non-transparent clothes that do not show the skin color underneath them is one of the obligations and conditions of the validity of the prayer ... the navel and knees are not part of the Awrah.

Source: Al-Mughni

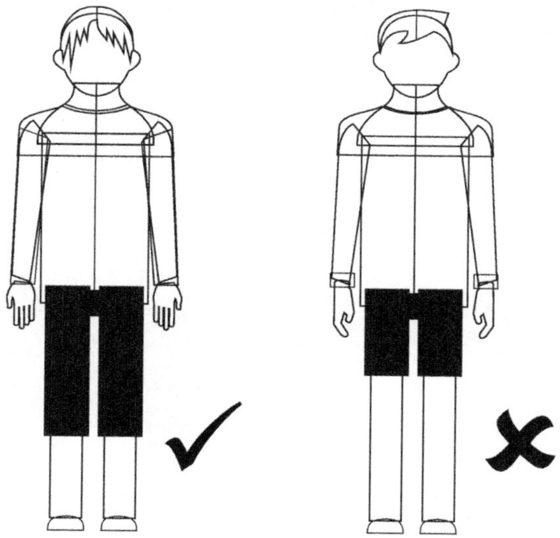

SINGING, MUSIC & DANCING

SINGING:

Shaykh al-Islam Ibn Taymiyyah said, discussing the state of the person who has gotten used to listening to singing: Hence you find that those who have gotten used to it and for whom it is like food and drink will never have the desire to listen to the Qur'aan or feel joy when they hear it, and they never find in listening to its verses the same feeling that they find when listening to poetry. Indeed, if they hear the Qur'aan, they hear it with an inattentive heart and talk whilst it is being recited, but if they hear whistling and clapping of hands, they lower their voices and keep still, and pay attention. *(Majmu' al-Fataawa, 11/557 ff)*

Some of the people say that singing is a form of worship if the intention is for it to help one to obey Allah!

Ibn al-Qayyim said: How strange! What type of faith, light, insight, guidance and knowledge can be gained from listening to tuneful verses and music in which most of what is said is Haraam and deserves the wrath and punishment of Allah and His Messenger? … How can anyone who has the least amount of insight and faith in his heart draw near to Allah and increase his faith by enjoying something which is hated by Him, and He detests the one who says it and the one who accepts it?

(Madaarij al-Saalikeen, 1/485)

MUSIC:

Difference between Listening and Hearing

Shaykh al-Islam (Ibn Taymiyah) said: Concerning (music) which a person does not intend to listen to there is no prohibition or blame, according to scholarly consensus. Hence blame or praise is connected to **listening**, not to hearing. The one who listens to the Qur'aan will be rewarded for it, whereas the one who hears it without intending or wanting to will not be rewarded for that, because actions are judged by intentions. The same applies to musical instruments which are forbidden: if a person hears them without intending to, that does not matter.

(al-Majmu', 10/78).

Shaykh Ibn 'Uthaymeen said:

The drum that is covered on both sides is called the tabl, and it is not permissible, because it is a kind of musical instrument and **all kinds of musical instruments are Haraam**, except that for which there is evidence that it is Halaal, which is the daff at weddings.

Fataawa Islamiyyah, 3/186.

Shaykh al-Islam Ibn Taymiyah said:

The view of the four imams is that all musical instruments are prohibited and none of the followers of the imams mentioned any dispute concerning musical instruments.

Majmoo' al-Fataawa (11/576, 577).

Ibn al-Qayyim said:
Anyone who has the slightest knowledge should not have any reservations about that – i.e., singing and musical instruments. The least that may be said is that it is the symbol of evildoers and drinkers of alcohol.

Ighaathat al-Lahfaan (1/228).

Al-Albaani said:
Hence the four madhhabs are agreed that all musical instruments are prohibited.

As-Silsilah as-Saheehah (1/145)

DANCING:
Shaykh Ibn 'Uthaymeen said:
Dancing is Makrooh in principle, but if it is done in the western manner or in imitation of the Kaafir women, then it becomes Haraam, because the Prophet ﷺ said: "Whoever imitates a people is one of them." Moreover, it sometimes leads to fitnah, because the dancer may be a young, beautiful woman, so the other women are tempted. Even if she is among other women, the other women may do things that indicate that they are tempted by her. And whatever is a cause of fitnah is not allowed.

Liqa' al-Baab al-Maftooh, q. 1085.

SMOKING

Smoking refers to the action of lighting a cigarette, a pipe, a cigar, a water pipe, or any other object made from tobacco or materials of similar effects. The object is then sucked on with the lips to extract smoke. This smoke is inhaled into the chest and then exhaled from the nose and mouth as a thick white smoke. "Smoking" is now used to refer to the action of producing this smoke in English, Arabic, and other languages.

Smoking contains poisonous materials, such as nicotine, tar, carbon monoxide, arsenic, benzopyrene, etc., that the smoker swallows in small proportions. Their harm accumulates with time to result in a gradual killing of the human organs and tissues.

Sheesha, Hookah, Argileh and smoking are all evil actions and are Haraam, because of the harm they cause to one's body and wealth. Allah, may He be exalted, said, describing our Prophet Muhammad ﷺ "he allows them as lawful At-Tayyibaat (i.e. all good and lawful as regards things, deeds, beliefs, persons and foods), and prohibits them as unlawful Al-Khabaaith (i.e. all evil and unlawful as regards things, deeds, beliefs, persons and foods)"

[Surah al-A'raaf 7:157].

It is proven that the Prophet ﷺ said: "There should be neither harm nor reciprocating harm." So, it is not permissible to use these things or to sell them or to distribute them.

Fataawa al-Lajnah al-Daimah, 26/351)
Shaykh Abdul-Azeez ibn Abdullaah Aal ash-Shaykh
Shaykh Abdullaah al-Ghudayyan
Shaykh Saaleh al-Fawzaan

Ruling on Electronic Cigarettes or Vapes

There is no distinction between the two in terms of the laws prohibiting them until it is established that these new types of cigarettes include hazardous ingredients and that the harm, they cause is the same as, similar to, or higher than that of regular cigarettes.

But if there are types that are proven, by means of examinations and laboratory tests carried out by trustworthy scientists, to contain natural flavorings only, and they do not contain any Haraam substances and are not harmful to the users or others, then in that case it is not Haraam to use these safe kinds. The ruling depends on whether the reason for it is present or not.

SOCIAL MEDIA

Today, the main uses of social media are sharing, learning, interacting, and marketing.

SHARING:

Bragging and showing off

Those who are afflicted with bragging and photographing his home furniture, his children's clothes, his car, his decorations, his travels, and what he ate and drank on social media.

Ibn Hazm Al-Andaloosee said:

How many have we not seen bragging about their possessions, it was lost due an envious eye or an enemy's plot. Guard against this attitude, it is harmful and completely useless.

End quote. Al-Akhlaaq wal-Siyar

Other dangers of sharing on social media:

Sharing images of your house or hobbies could unintentionally alert those who want to steal your costly possessions—like art, jewels, gadgets, or desired collections—that you have them. Posting images from your current travel could let criminals know that you are currently away from home. Photos or information about family members could expose their identities, locations, or potentially make them targets.

LEARNING:

Social media, when used in a responsible and age-appropriate way, can help children learn, think critically and build the skills they need for the future. It helps Muslims learn the basics of religion without any obstruction. Social media can help one learn affairs such as Aqeedah, the meaning & conditions. Nullifiers of the Shahaadah, memorization of the Qur'aan and concise books of Sunnah & Tawheed.

SUICIDE

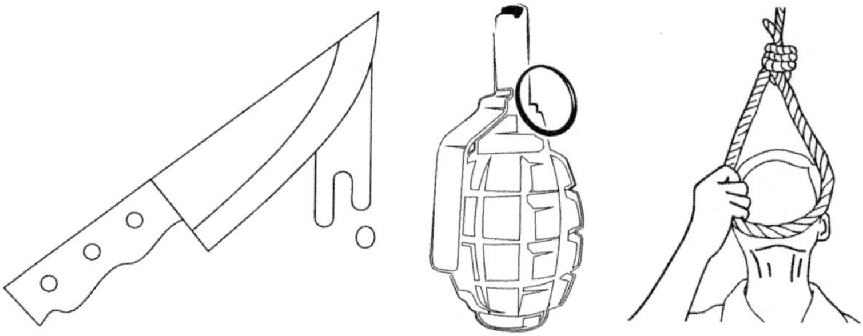

Suicide is a great evil, and it is a sin from the major sins. It is not permissible for a Muslim to commit Suicide. The Prophet ﷺ stated that the one who commits suicide will be punished with something like that with which he killed himself.

Abu Hurayrah narrated that the Prophet ﷺ said: "Whoever throws himself down from a mountain and kills himself will be in the Fire of Hell, throwing himself down therein for ever and ever. Whoever takes poison and kills himself, his poison will be in his hand and he will be sipping it in the Fire of Hell for ever and ever. Whoever kills himself with a piece of iron, that piece of iron will be in his hand and he will be stabbing himself in the stomach with it in the Fire of Hell, for ever and ever."

Narrated by al-Bukhaari, 5442; Muslim, 109.

The risk of suicide increases greatly when kids and teens have access to firearms at home, and nearly 60% of all suicides in the United States are committed with a gun. Suicide rates differ between boys and girls. Girls think about and attempt suicide about twice as often as boys, and tend to attempt suicide by overdosing on drugs or cutting themselves. Yet boys die by suicide about four times as often girls, and experts think this is because they tend to use more lethal methods.

Teenagers with mental health problems — such as anxiety, depression, bipolar disorder and those who are bullied are at greater risk of suicidal thoughts. It was found that the Muslim population showed a lower rate of suicide in comparison to individuals from other religions, and religious individuals showed faster recovery from suicidal ideation.

Source: Mental Health, Religion and Suicide. Open Journal of Medical Psychology.

The religiously committed Muslim does not see suicide as an option

What drives a Muslim to commit suicide?

1. Lack of knowledge and a proper understanding of Islamic religion.
2. Weak or no belief in the Day of Judgment.
3. Strong cultural influence.
4. Overindulgence in TV dramas/serials that encourage suicide has a negative impact on people with weak minds.

TATTOOS

What is the purpose of tattoos?
They include religious purposes, for protection or as a source of power, as an indication of group membership, as a status symbol, as an artistic expression, for permanent cosmetics, and as an adjunct to reconstructive surgery.

Tattooing has been around since the earliest known societies. Heavily associated with such pagan cultures, it typically involved propitiating the gods or either summoning or warding off demonic forces.

All kind of tattoos, regardless of whether they are painful or not, are considered Haraam. The creation of Allah is altered by tattooing. The tattoo artist and the person getting one are both cursed.

Abd-Allah ibn Mas'ood said: "May Allah curse the women who do tattoos and those for whom tattoos are done, those who pluck their eyebrows and those who file their teeth for the purpose of beautification and alter the creation of Allah."

Al-Bukhaari, al-Libas, 5587; Muslim, al-Libas, 5538

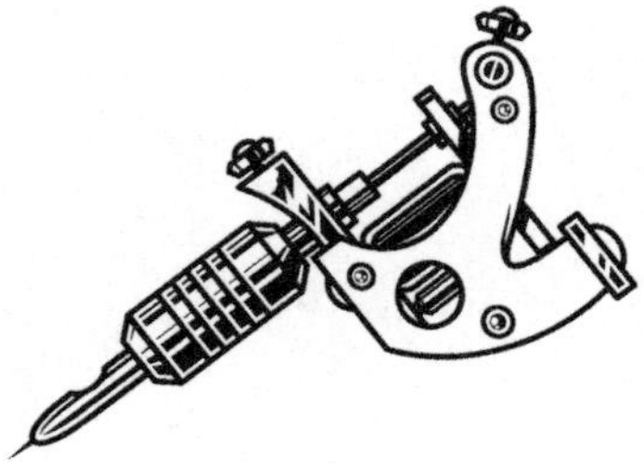

VACATIONS

Islam came to change many of the distorted concepts that are held by imperfect human minds.

Shaykh Saaleh al-Fawzaan said:
Travelling to the lands of Kuffaar is not permissible, because there are many dangers posed to one's beliefs and morals by mixing with the Kuffaar and staying among them. But if there is a valid need and a sound purpose for travelling, such as travelling for medical treatment that is not available in a Muslim country, or travelling to study something that is not available in a Muslim country, or travelling for business purposes, these are valid purposes for which it is permissible to travel to Non-Muslim countries, provided that one adheres to the rituals of Islam and is able to carry out his religious duties in that country, but that (travel) should be done only as much as is necessary, then one should return to the Muslim world.

As for travelling for tourism, that is not permissible, because the Muslim has no need of that and it does not serve any interest that matches or outweighs the harm and danger to his religious commitment and beliefs that it involves.

Al-Muntaqa min Fataawa al-Shaykh al-Fawzaan (2/question no. 221)

So how about tourism that encourages sin and immorality, beaches where there are thousands of women & men who are virtually naked, and men mix freely with women, and is organized in order to promote it and spread it?

It is not permissible to go to places of corruption for the sake of tourism, because of the danger that poses to one's religious commitment and morals. Islam came to block the means that lead to evil.

Fataawa al-Lajnah al-Daa'imah (26/332).

VIOLENT BEHAVIOR

Violent behavior is any behavior by an individual that threatens or actually harms or injures the individual or others or destroys property. Violent behavior often begins with verbal threats but over time escalates to involve physical harm.

As a general rule, Muslims should not harm other people, especially other Muslims. The only exception to this rule is due to the need for self-defense against aggression or to avert some greater evil.

Narrated by Abu Sirmah, the Messenger of Allah ﷺ said: "Whoever harms others, Allah will harm him; and whoever causes hardship to others, Allah will cause hardship to him."

Al-Albaani classed it as Hasan in Saheeh at-Tirmidhi.

Narrated Abu Musa:
Some people asked Allah's Apostle, "Whose Islam is the best? He replied, "One who avoids harming the Muslims with his tongue and hands."

Al-Bukhaari, Volume 1, Book 2, Number 10

Allah, may He be exalted, says (interpretation of the meaning): "And never think that Allah is unaware of what the wrongdoers do. He only delays them for a Day when eyes will stare [in horror]"

[Surah Ibraaheem 14:42].

RECKLESS DRIVING

Reckless driving is a serious offense that can result in devastating injuries and even death, in some cases. This type of traffic violation typically occurs when a driver displays complete and utter disregard for traffic lights, signs, and signals made by other drivers.

Shaykh Ibn 'Uthaymeen issued a Fatwa stating that it is not permissible to run a red light. He regarded that as coming under the heading of obeying the authorities, which is obligatory, because Allah says (interpretation of the meaning):

"O you who believe! Obey Allah and obey the Messenger, and those of you (Muslims) who are in authority" [al-Nisa' 4:59].

Liqaa'aat al-Baab il-Maftooh (3/178), question no. 1265

Some reckless driving behaviors come from driver inexperience and peer pressure – especially among teen drivers. Young or new drivers may not understand the dangers of willful or wanton driving offenses such as speeding.

GLOSSARY

Aayah: *pl. aayaat.* Sign, miracle, example, lesson, verse.

Abd: *pl.* ebaad. slave, servant, worshipper.

Adhaan: the call to prayer.

Bid'ah: innovation, that which is newly introduced into the religion of Allah.

Da'eef: weak. A hadeeth that has failed to meet the criteria of authenticity.

Deen: religion, way of life.

Dhaalim: one who commits dhulm: injustice, harm, transgression either against Allah, himself or another creation.

Dhikr: remembrance, making mention of Allah.

Du'aa: supplication, invocation.

Eemaan: faith that also comprises a meaning of submission. Its place is the heart, the tongue and the limbs and it increases with obedience and decreases with disobedience.

Faqeeh: *pl. fuqahaa:* an expert in Islamic law, a Legal Jurist.

Fard: see waajib.

Fasaad: corruption, decay, and invalidity.

Fatwa: *pl. fataawa:* legal ruling.

Fiqh: understanding and comprehension of the rulings and legislation of Islam.

Fisq: *pl. fusooq:* Immorality, transgression, wickedness.

Fitnah: *pl. fitan:* trial, tribulation, civil strife.

Fitrah: primordial nature, the harmony between man, creation and Creator.

Ghayb: the Unseen, those matters beyond our senses.

Haafidh: *pl. huffaadh:* Hadeeth Master, commonly referred to one who has memorized at least 100,000 ahaadeeth.

Hadeeth: *pl. ahaadeeth:* speech, report. A narration describing the sayings, actions, character, physical description and tacit approval of the Prophet ﷺ.

Hajj: pilgrimage, one of the pillars of Islam.

Halaal: permissible.

Haraam: forbidden, sacred, restricted. Unlawful, that which the legally responsible person is rewarded for leaving and sinful for doing.

Hasan: good: a hadeeth that has met the criteria of authenticity to a sufficient level as would allow it to be used as legal proof.

Ijtihaad: striving and exerting: striving to attain the Islamic ruling on an issue, after certain preconditions have been met by the person.

Imaam: model, religious leader, one who leads the congregational prayer or leads a community.

Isnaad: chain of narration.

Jaahiliyyah: Pre-Islamic Ignorance. Technically this refers to the condition of a people before the guidance of Allah reaches them, or the state of a people that prevents them from accepting the guidance of Allah.

Janaabah: state of major impurity.

Janaazah: funeral prayer, funeral procession.

Jihaad: striving in the way of Allah to make His Word supreme.

Jinn: another creation besides mankind who are invisible to us. They are also subject to the laws of Islam and will be judged in the Hereafter according to how they lived in this life.

Kaafir: a rejecter of faith, disbeliever.

Khateeb: one who delivers lectures, one who delivers the Friday sermon.

Khawf: fear.

Khutbah: sermon, lecture, Friday sermon.

Mufassir: *pl. mufassiroon:* Exegete, commentator, one who explains the Qur'aan.

Muhaajir: *pl. muhaajiroon:* One who performs hijrah. The Companions who migrated from Makkah to Madeenah.

Muhaddith: *pl. muhaddithoon:* Scholar of Hadeeth.

Muhkam: clear and definitive. An aayah of the Qur'aan that carries a clear and conclusive meaning.

Mujtahid: one who performs ijtihaad. That level of scholar who can deduce independent verdicts directly from the primary Islamic sources.

Mustahabb: recommended, that which a legally responsible person is rewarded for doing but not sinful for leaving.

Mukallaf: morally responsible person.

Mulhid: heretic.

Munaafiq: hypocrite, one who outwardly displays Islam but inwardly conceals disbelief. This is the worst type of hypocrisy and its possessor is the worst type of disbeliever, there are other lesser types.

Qadar: Allah's decree of all matters in accordance with His prior knowledge and as dictated by His wisdom.

Qiblah: direction to which the Muslims pray, towards the ka'bah.

Qiyaas: Analogy.

Riyaa: an act of worship undertaken by someone to be seen and praised by others and not purely for Allah.

Ruqyaa: recitation used to cure an illness or disease. It can only be done in the Arabic tongue, in words whose meaning is understood, using verses of the Qur'aan or supplications of the Prophet combined with the belief that it is only Allah who in reality gives the cure.

Sabr: patience, steadfastness.

Saheeh: healthy, sound, authentic, correct. A hadeeth that has met the criteria of authenticity and can be used as a legal proof.

Salaah: the second pillar of Islam, the prayer.

Salaf: predecessors, commonly employed to refer to the first three generations of Muslims.

Sawm: fasting, one of the pillars of Islam.

Shahaadah: testification, witness. The declaration that none has the right to be worshipped save Allah and that Muhammad ﷺ is the Messenger of Allah.

Sharee'ah: divine Islamic law as ordained by Allah.

Shareek: partner, associate.

Shaykh: old man, learned person, scholar.

Shaytaan: Satan, Iblees, a devil.

Shirk: polytheism, associating partners with Allah in matters that are exclusive to Allah.

Sunan: a compilation of ahaadeeth.

Sunnah: habit, customary practice, norm and usage as sanctioned by tradition. The sayings, commands, prohibitions, actions, and tacit approvals of the Prophet ﷺ.

Surah: chapter of the Qur'aan.

Taaghoot: all that is falsely worshipped besides Allah.

Tafseer: elucidation, clarification, explanation of the Qur'aan.

Tawakkul: trust and absolute reliance.

Tawheed: the foundation stone of Islam, the absolute belief in the Oneness of Allah - His being the sole Creator and Sustainer, His being the only One deserving worship and His being unique with respect to His Names and Attributes.

Ummah: nation, the Muslim nation.

Waajib: obligatory that which a legally responsible person is rewarded for doing and sinful for leaving. In the eyes of the majority waajib has the same meaning as fard.

Wudu: ritual ablution.

Zakaah: one of the pillars of Islam, an obligatory tax levied on a Muslim wealth subject to certain criteria.

Zuhd: asceticism.